W9-DHF-989

Child of
the Owl

Laurence Yep

• • • •

With
Connected Readings

PRENTICE HALL
Upper Saddle River, New Jersey
Needham, Massachusetts
Glenview, Illinois

Copyright © 2000 by Prentice-Hall, Inc., Upper Saddle River, New Jersey 07458. All rights reserved. No part of this book may be reproduced or transmitted in any form or by any means, electronic or mechanical, including photocopying, recording, or by any information storage and retrieval system, without permission in writing from the publisher. Printed in the United States of America.

ISBN 0-13-437497-5

2 3 4 5 6 7 8 9 10   03 02 01 00

PRENTICE HALL

Acknowledgments

Grateful acknowledgment is made to the following for permission to reprint copyrighted material:

Chelsea House Publishers
"A Nation of Nations" by Senator Daniel Patrick Moynihan from *The Peoples of North America: The Chinese Americans* by William Daley. Copyright © 1987 by Chelsea House Publishers, a division of Main Line Book Co. Reprinted by permission of Chelsea House Publishers.

Lucha Corpi
"Voices" by Lucha Corpi, translated by Catherine Rodriguez-Nieto. First printed in *Variations on a Storm* (Berkeley: Third Woman Press, 1990).

Joyce Hansen
"New Day Dawning" by Joyce Hansen. Copyright © 1996 by Joyce Hansen, from *But That's Another Story*, edited by Sandy Asher. Reprinted by permission of the author.

HarperCollins Publishers
Child of the Owl by Laurence Yep. Copyright © 1977 by Laurence Yep. "Prayer" from *Brown Angels: An Album of Pictures and Verse* by Walter Dean Myers. Copyright © 1993 by Walter Dean Myers. Used by permission of HarperCollins Publishers. From *Thief of Hearts* by Laurence Yep. Copyright © 1995 Laurence Yep.

Meriwether Publishing Ltd.
"Grandma Thinks I'm Beautiful" from *Acting Natural* by Peg Kehret. © copyright 1991 by Meriwether Publishing Ltd. Reprinted by permission of Meriwether Publishing Ltd. Colorado Springs, CO 80907.

(Acknowledgments continue on p. 191.)

Contents

Child of the Owl
Laurence Yep

Connected Readings

Child of the Owl

Child of the Owl

Laurence Yep

Chapter One

August 1964

IT was hard to understand Barney with the air tubes up his nose. It made his voice sound funny and he couldn't talk very loud. There was a cast on one arm and one leg too and bandages on the others. And his hands were still—that was the worst of it. Barney had long, nervous hands that were usually drumming out a tune or scratching his arm or doing something, but now they were quiet. They didn't seem to belong to him.

I just stood in the doorway because I didn't want to bother Barney if he was about to take a nap. But I didn't like looking at him too much so I looked around the ward. Almost every other patient there had flowers or baskets of fruit or little transistor radios or their own little electric clocks: something that made the space around their bed their own. And most everyone had some visitors with them. Even the oldest guys in there had some friends visiting them. But Barney had nothing and no one, except for me.

"Casey?" Barney's voice sounded muffled and more nasal.

"Hey, Barney." I tried to smile as I walked over to his bed. Someone had taken the visitor's chair that ought to have been by his bedside so I had to stand up. My sweat shirt was the kind that had the pockets in front so you could stick your hands in them to warm up. Barney always said it made me look like a kangaroo in jeans.

"What are you doing here?" Barney asked. "Thought they wouldn't let kids in?"

"Snuck in. I had Morey draw me a map of where your bed was on this floor and then I snuck up the stairs."

"How'd you get past the nurses at the desk?"

"Morey's talking to them. You know how hard it is to get away from old Morey once he grabs hold of you." I pulled the two Peter Paul bars out of my sweat shirt. "Thought your sweet tooth might be bothering you." I glanced at the big fat Whitman's Sampler of chocolate Barney's neighbor had. "Sorry it couldn't be a whole boxful."

" 'S all right. Can't eat them anyway. Put them in the drawer, will you?" Barney waved his hand vaguely toward the nightstand.

I opened up the little drawer there and put the two bars in beside the wash cloth and the bar of soap. "It's just as well." I tried to laugh in a relaxed way. "They got a little soft from being in my pockets. They'll cool off this way."

But when I'd finished closing the drawer and turned back to Barney, I saw he was looking at me in this funny way like I'd never seen before, not in all our years together. He looked real sad and scared at the same time. "You ain't too mad at me, are you, baby?"

"Mad?" I asked, surprised. "Why should I be mad?"

"I mean about me losing the money and all."

"The only guys I'm mad at are the guys who beat you up and robbed you when you left the bookie."

Barney turned his face up toward the ceiling. He seemed relieved. "You're not any madder than me. I was already seeing us on that Greyhound . . . no, a chauffeured limousine down to San Francisco."

I can't remember when Barney's story began but all my life I'd heard this story about how this little girl and her father were going to hit it big one of these days, either in his gambling or in one of his real-estate deals that one of his drinking buddies was going to set up—Barney was always their bosom buddy till the deal fell through.

And then he'd tell me how he was going to get that big penthouse apartment on Nob Hill over in San Francisco so we could see the fog coming in over the city and then we'd turn around and look across the bay at the lights of Oakland, strung out like a shimmering golden river. And I wouldn't stop buying clothes, toys, comics, and records I wanted till I had filled up that apartment. And then we'd move to another. Somehow Barney never got around to what would happen after we ran out of things to buy and apartments to move into. But maybe that's because his story never really got off the ground.

I guess there used to be a mom, Jeanie by name, in the story too, but she must have dropped out of it quick because she died when I was small. I don't remember her, though I've got a photo of her taken when Barney still had some hair. It was at some party and she was the pretty, smiling girl sitting next to Barney in his army uniform after he got back from World War II. Both of them held up plastic champagne glasses that didn't have champagne in them, only Schlitz.

4

When we were really desperate for money—usually a week after Barney had to pawn his wedding ring again—Barney would take up his hobby, which most other people would call *work*, until he had paid our bills and re-claimed his ring. In Fresno he was a dishwasher and in Redding he was a waiter—at the Tokyo Palace no less because Redding is a small town short on Orientals and no one read the part of the menu in Japanese much less ordered in it—and in Santa Barbara he was a fry cook at a Big Boy with a chef's hat and a red neckerchief.

And then came Stockton when we were living in this tacky hotel because the latest of Barney's mobile junk heaps that slick dealers always conned Barney into thinking were cars—well, that particular junk heap died more quickly than usual. Barney got a job dishwashing and I got into the local school and we settled down for a while, but Barney got to telling the story more and more and that was a bad sign and the next paycheck Barney took over to the local bookie to try his luck on the horses. He used the date of my birthday, the twenty-third, to pick out the number of the horse like he usually did and even though it was a long twenty-to-one, he plunked his whole paycheck down. For once . . . for once in his life Barney hit it big and he could see his story coming true. Even when he had paid off Big Mike, the bookie, he had a lot left over. Only Barney never made it out of the alley, where some losers had waited for him.

Right then Barney looked so down that I reached over and patted his hand. Usually Barney and me didn't go in for that father and daughter stuff and go around hugging and kissing like a lot of other people. But this was different. "Hey, Barney, it's okay. We'll do that when we can really go down in style. The important thing is that your luck's starting to turn around."

Barney turned his head on the pillow and winked at me. "That's right, baby. And next time I'm not gonna tackle some two-bit outfit like Big Mike's. Next time I'm gonna take on Vegas."

That sounded more like the old Barney. I gave his hand a squeeze and let go. "Sure. Why use up your string of luck on guys like Big Mike?"

"Meantime, I want you to keep my luck warm for me. It's in my pants in the closet over there." Barney's bed was the closest to the wall where there was a row of tall, narrow wooden closets. I opened the first one and saw his old work pants hanging up there with his torn shirt. Someone, maybe one of the nurses, had washed the blood stains off of it. I fished the little fat, bald, smiling man out of Barney's pocket. Barney didn't know anything more about the little man than what was stamped into the plastic of his back: *Happy God—Souvenir of Chinatown*. (When you turned it over, though, the bottom was stamped: *Made in Hoboken*.) He'd bought it a long time ago when he used to live in San Francisco.

"But he's your luck, Barney," I said.

"He'll just get cold here, baby. He's gotta be kept snug and warm someplace. So you keep him for me."

Barney normally didn't let it out of his pocket so I knew he must be up to something. Still, to please him, I stuffed it inside one of my sweat-shirt pockets. "Moe's been letting me wash dishes in the back so with that and the paper-route money, we're doing pretty good." Actually, we were doing better than ever because Barney usually gambled or loaned or got cheated out of most of that money so we were always left at the end of the month scrambling around for some way to pay our bills.

"That's no good, baby. My kid's hands were made for better things. And it's too heavy for you."

"I'm twelve." I shrugged, annoyed.

"Sure, baby. Sure. But why kill yourself up here when you can stay with your mom's folks? You remember her older brother, that big-shot lawyer?"

"Phil the Pill? Yeah, I remember him." He'd bought me a glass of milk and Barney a cup of coffee and acted like he was giving us the crown jewels. "I don't want to go live with them."

"It's just temporary, baby," he said. "Just temporary. You know. Till I get on my feet again."

That was why he'd given me the luck charm. It was about the only thing of value—and that wasn't much—that he had to give me. I put my foot on the metal railing on the side of his bed. "You trying to get rid of me, Barney?"

Barney got mad then. "You know that ain't true, baby. I'm just thinking of you. It's just that . . . well, hell . . . I worry about you."

"I'm not the one that got beat up." I brushed back the hair from my face. "I told you that Big Mike's place was in a bad part of town."

"Baby, there ain't no bookie gonna be in a good one. But it'd be a big load off my mind if I knew you were in a big house in a nice neighborhood. And it's the end of August so you'd be able to start school down there."

"But if I stayed up here in Stockton," I argued hopefully, "I could sneak up here and bring you candy and racing forms."

"Morey can do that. Come on. How about doing like I ask?" Barney's voice had taken on this wheedling tone, like when he was trying to hit somebody for a ten spot he needed really bad and knew he was only going to get a fin, or only a one, or even worse, nothing. I'd seen that happen so many times I couldn't turn Barney down now when he was using that tone on me.

I glanced at him suspiciously. "You promise it's only temporary?"

"Of course, it's only temporary, baby. I'm your father for Chrissake. Haven't I always been taking care of you all these years?"

It was more like the other way around, but it didn't seem polite to say so. "Okay, but it's only temporary."

"Thanks, baby. You'll see. We'll be back together again before you know it. I got this feeling, you know?"

I sighed. "Yeah, Barney. I know."

At that moment the nurse came in. I'd give you five-to-three odds that she wore army-surplus underwear and had sergeant's stripes tattooed on her arm. She even looked just like that fat, potato-nosed Sergeant Snorkel in the Beetle Bailey comic strip. Morey came in right behind her. He shrugged apologetically. He'd stalled her as long as he could.

"What are you doing here?" the nurse demanded. "Children are not allowed to visit."

"She's no child," Barney said. "She's a midget." I ignored Barney, pretending instead to be surprised.

"Oh, you mean this isn't the Greyhound terminal?" I asked innocently.

"This is a hospital and you know it." The nurse crossed her arms. I'd give you ten to one that she strangled bears for fun.

"Gee, I was wondering why there weren't any buses."

The nurse gave her head a stern little shake. "*Mister Young,* we simply cannot turn this ward into a nursery."

"I never saw this kid before in my life till she came in pestering everybody about the next bus to Frisco." Barney gave her his twenty-carat, sincere look—the one he wore on those rare occasions when he went job hunting, usually right after some bookie's goons had just threatened to break his legs unless he paid off part of what he owed.

But the nurse couldn't tell that Barney was pulling her leg. "You are the only Chinese on this floor."

I pretended to stare down at Barney in horror. "Gosh, I hope it isn't catching."

The nurse's mouth moved up and down for a while and I thought, what the hell. "Bye, Barn." I bent over and kissed the one unbandaged, unbruised spot on Barney's cheek. "See ya later."

"You go see your mom's folks like I tole you," he said.

And Nurse Snorkel started right in on Barney. "Now see here, Mister Young, we can't have your daughter running around the hospital."

"She's like an act of God, nurse. I got as much control over her as I do over the rain." Barney managed to wink an eye under the bandage encasing the top of his head. I figured he'd be okay so I winked back and slipped out into the hall with Morey.

Morey was this old musician with a skin like brown velvet. When the light shone on it, his skin gleamed gold. Most of the time he slopped around in an old flannel shirt and army fatigue pants, but when he really wanted to dress up—like today—he put on this old zoot suit of his which was what they were wearing twenty or twenty-five years ago. It's a suit with shoulders padded like a football player's—a man looks twice as wide—and with big, floppy pants narrowing at the leg and a big, broad-brimmed hat with a small crown, and the suit and hat were a bright pink. With that he wore a pair of bright patent-leather, black-and-pink shoes, and he swung a key chain as he walked.

We took off down the corridor past the startled nurses and got into the elevator. I was glad of that. It wasn't any fun sneaking up four flights of stairs into Barney's ward.

"Morey," I asked him, "do you really think Barney'll get better?"

"Oh, that cat'll be upright before you know it." Morey's voice was like an instrument all by itself, well oiled and rich, that wheedled the music out of his every breath. "Hey, you gonna do like he says?"

I suppose Barney and Morey had talked about it the night before.

"But I can't leave Barney alone. You know that."

"Who's he gonna shoot craps with? Big Mama? He's got enough worries without wondering about you."

"I've been taking care of us all this time. I ought to be able to take care of myself. I mean, we'll lose our paper routes." Barney and I had a morning as well as an evening paper route. That was how we got our eating money. And then with what odd jobs

Barney could get and occasional wins, we paid our rent—sometimes. A lot of times, though, we just had to skip out of the hotel because Barney bet all our money on some sure thing which usually was only sure to lose.

As we got out of the elevator into the lobby, Morey shook his head. "Hey, slick chick. I'll take over running them."

"You won't get up early enough."

"Well, 'bout time I did. Gonna start me a new life. Get me some gigs. Next thing you know Ole Morey'll be cruising down to the City to pick you up in his shiny new Cadillac Coup de-veel."

"Moe says Lincolns are better." Moe was the owner of the greasy-spoon joint where Barney worked off and on. Moe stayed our friend, mainly because I saw to it that Barney never borrowed money from him.

Morey curled his lip up scornfully. "What would that cat know about class? His idea of class is his ole baby shoes hanging over the mirror."

"Well, how are we gonna pay for the hospital unless I get a job someplace?"

"Installments, baby. Installments. You don't gotta pay it all off right now. Just a little at a time. Now here." He picked up my hand, turning it palm upwards, and slapped twenty dollars down on it. "Here's money for the bus and a little besides so you can show your cousins you ain't no poor trash."

"Morey, you hocked your horn," I accused him.

"I'll get it back, baby. Always do. Now you do like Barney says."

I gave Morey a hug. "And we'll pay you back just as soon as we hit it big."

"What am I going to need that money for? I'm gonna hit it big myself and then you and your old man kin be my guests at the front-row, cen-ter ta-ble," he said, relishing every syllable of the last few words. "Meantime, you have some fun meeting your mom's folks, you hear?"

"Yeah," I grinned, "I hear."

II

IT wasn't fun like Morey said. Not at all.

I suppose Barney had wheedled one of the nurses into calling from the hospital so Phil was expecting my collect call. He didn't sound all that thrilled either, but he told me to come on down. But, boy, he sounded like a real pill.

Phil was Mom's oldest brother and the big success in the family—a hotshot lawyer with a fancy house in the St. Francis Woods section of San Francisco. He was a short, round man with a flat top and big horn-rimmed glasses that were always flecked with dandruff and dust so he saw the world a little fuzzy. He didn't seem to notice me when I got off the Greyhound. Instead he kept on standing on tiptoe, craning his head up so he could try and see through the rest of the people getting off the bus.

"Hey, are you my uncle?"

He ignored me, probably hoping that some little girl with bouncy curls and a frilly, pink party dress would get off the bus instead. Well, I'm one of those people who think that you ought to get what you deserve, or I wouldn't have swung my duffel bag lightly against his knee. "Hey, are you my Uncle Phil?"

Phil the Pill sighed as the bus driver got off and slammed the door shut. It was obvious there was no one else on the bus, and no other Chinese but me. He looked at me. "You're not Jeanie's kid?" he asked, hoping against hope.

"In person." I tried to smile. He was putting me up for a while, after all.

"Did you check your luggage on the bus?" Phil started looking around for the bus driver so he could unlock the luggage compartment below on the right side of the bus.

"I got my stuff." I held Barney's old, beat-up, brown duffel bag.

Phil didn't say anything—just turned away. I followed him out to his car—a whalelike, gold Lincoln Continental that he'd left double-parked outside the terminal.

"Aren't you afraid of getting a ticket?" I asked.

"The traffic cop around here knows me," he said. "This is near the city-hall beat." He fished out a key chain that must have been covered by two inches' worth of keys to honorary brotherhoods and fraternities: Rotarians, Kiwanis, Odd Fellows and so on—I knew about honorary keys because I'd seen them once in a pawnshop when I went in with Barney. He unlocked the trunk. I could have stuffed the corpse of a baby elephant and its trainer into that trunk. I put my duffel bag inside and it looked awful small and forlorn in there. I suppose Phil had cleaned out the trunk for my luggage and stuff. He slammed the trunk lid shut and then went over to the driver's side, opened it, and reached in. The button popped up on my side and the window rolled down. I wouldn't have been surprised if the door had opened by itself and started playing "The Star-Spangled Banner." I mean, that car had everything: power steering, power brakes, powered windows, air conditioning, stereo AM-FM, tinted windshields, and even a pair of little, white baby booties with a big script *P* initialed on the toes, dangling from the stem of the front-view mirror.

"Whose are those?" I pointed to the booties as I slid in.

"They belong to Pam-Pam. That's what we call Pamela, your cousin," he explained. "She's about the same age as you. We bought a pair of booties for you too when you were born. They had a *C* on them."

I suppose you can't help wearing stuff like that when you're only a baby; but thank God Barney had the good taste to chuck them out—or sell them more likely—when I didn't need them anymore. Then I reminded myself that it wasn't fair to Phil to think that way. After all, he'd given them to me as a gift and he was putting me up for about a month or two—I figured that it would take that long for Barney to get back on his feet.

It wasn't much better when I hit *Chez Phil the Pill.* There wasn't one cheap piece of furniture or painting in the place but it was all kind of, I don't know, kind of impersonal. Like it had all been ordered out of a Sears catalogue because that was what every other lawyer of fifty thousand a year ordered from San Francisco to Bangor. But the only difference between Phil's stuff and the stuff in the cheap furnished rooms where Barney and me lived was the price tag, not the taste. Instead of ordering the twenty-dollar dresser like you'd find in one of our rooms, Phil ordered the two-hundred-dollar dresser. Not because he liked it, but because it had the right price tag.

The only thing in Phil's house without an expensive price tag was me, and they started to see what they could do about upping *my* value as soon as I got in the door. "Oh," said Ethel in a real small voice. Ethel was Phil's wife. "I think some of Pam-Pam's old dresses would fit her."

"Hi, Ethel." I stuffed my hands into my pockets and hunched my shoulders. "And I don't wear dresses. They just get in your way when you're trying to run away from the muggers."

"Oh," Ethel said in an even smaller, distressed voice. She actually believed me.

"Is that her? Is that her?" this little girl squealed. And Pam-Pam came flouncing down the stairs. And she *did* have her hair in curls and she *did* wear a pink, frilly dress. She slowed down, though, as she neared the bottom of the stairs. She clung to the railing, leaning her side against it, as if she needed some support. "Is that Casey?" She spoke in this breathless little-girl voice—not a real little girl, but like what she thought little girls ought to sound like. It was hard to realize we were about the same age.

Ethel turned around, trying to smile. "Pam-Pam, dear, come and meet your cousin Casey."

Pam-Pam didn't say anything. She just leaned a little harder against the railing.

Phil spoke very slowly as if he wanted to make sure they caught his words. "I thought that Casey could sleep in Annette's room."

"But we moved the bed into . . ." Ethel let her words drop off. "Oh, yes, of course." From the look of relief on Pam-Pam's face I guessed I was originally supposed to sleep in her room—only Phil didn't think I was the best influence upon a tender, impressionable child.

"Mo-ther," said a voice from the room that must have been the living room. "Mo-ther. You *simply* can not do that." A girl in her teens or early twenties shuffled out in big, fluffy household slippers and a flowered, quilted robe. The top part of her head was hidden by big, pink curlers so that it looked like the back of her head was being humped by a hedgehog. She was Annette, the oldest of Phil's kids and a junior over at Berkeley, where she was the president of the Chinese girls' sorority. As near as I could ever find out, she was studying to be Queen of the World. The Hedgehog shuffled up to Ethel. "Mo-ther. I *do not* have the room in my closet for somebody else's things."

"Oh, now, dear," Ethel coaxed, "you could have some of the room in our closet to put away some of the things that you don't use all the time—"

"I won't take up much room." I held up my duffel bag.

The Hedgehog turned around finally and saw me for the first time. Her nostrils flared and she turned back to Ethel. "Mo-ther. Really." She spoke in a quiet, deeply injured tone.

"Now. Now," Phil said. "We all have to make some sacrifices. I told Jeanie I'd look after her daughter and—"

"Why is it always me that has to put up with things?" The Hedgehog stormed up the steps.

Phil rubbed his forehead. "Ethel, go up and explain things to Annette, will you?"

Ethel seemed relieved to go up the steps away from me.

"Hey, listen. I could sleep on the sofa if you've got one."

"You're sleeping on a real bed," Phil insisted. "I told Jeanie I'd take care of you."

The next day, I put on one of Pam-Pam's old dresses because it seemed to make Ethel feel better—only at first Pam-Pam didn't want to give it up until Ethel reminded her that Phil had told Jeanie he'd take care of me, like I was an old geranium dying in its pot.

Actually, Phil treated me as if I was almost as helpless as a dying geranium. That afternoon I found out I could only watch wholesome television shows—travelogues and educational shows about how to stuff a mongoose. I put up with that for three days and then I tried to turn to a showing of *Dracula* on the tube. Phil the Pill got up from his easy chair, where he was reading *The Wall Street Journal*, and turned it off. "We do not," he informed me, "watch such trash in this house."

"Hey, but this isn't some cheapie horror flick. This is early Bela Lugosi. Barney and me always see it if there's a TV in the hotel lobby and we can get the other people to watch it."

Phil took a little breath and squared his shoulders. "I have no doubt that Barney lets you watch that seamy violence. He's just the type to enjoy it too. But it's a proven fact that young, maturing minds should not be exposed to such ugly fantasy."

"Who says so?"

Phil looked shocked. "Why, psychologists do."

"Which psychologists? I knew a psychologist once who loved it. He said Bela reminded him of his brother-in-law. And what's more he said that you couldn't find two psychologists who agreed with each other just like you couldn't find two bartenders who could make gimlets the same."

Phil the Pill raised his eyebrows. "I hardly think that some psychologist living in a skid-row hotel is a reputable authority."

"As a matter of fact, Barney and me were painting his study. And he was the head of the clinic at a big state hospital." And I left the room before Phil could think of something else to say.

Three days later, Ethel took Pam-Pam down to buy some school clothes and to show me the sights. Only I didn't think the dress departments of different stores were very scenic so while we were at the Emporium, I scribbled a note telling Ethel I'd see her at home. I slipped it into the pocket of her coat, which she had draped over a chair while she watched Pam-Pam trying on dresses. The chair was to the side away from the mirrors where they were so they didn't see me at all. Then I went off on my own, walking on down Market all the way to the Ferry Building. There weren't any more ferries but there were neat

three-dimensional maps of California. I could just make out
Stockton. Then I walked back up the other side of Market, stopping by these racks of comics and newspapers outside of a big,
fancy bank. There wasn't any newspaper booth, just the racks
that the owner must have put away every day.

The owner was a little dwarf, with an almost normal size
trunk but short, squat legs. He wore rimless glasses and a
funny little straw hat shaped like a fedora. He wore a green-
colored apron with pockets jingling with change.

"Eddy, what're you doing down here?"

He tilted up his head and studied me through the bottom half
of his bifocals. "Jesu Christ, you're Barney's kid, ain't you?"

"Yeah, I'm Casey. Remember me?" I felt warm inside at meeting an old face in a strange city.

"Sure, I do. You used to buy the racing sheets every day for
your dad. He still in San Mateo?"

"Naw. We're in Stockton checking out things right now. Only
he got hurt so I got to stay with some of my mom's folks."

We talked on for a little while. He used to run a small news-
stand in a little city down the peninsula near the fleatrap hotel
where we were staying. But he'd sold that and opened up this
place. We swapped memories for a while. I think he was lonely
himself, because he'd just come to the city a year ago. When I
left him, he told me to take my pick of the comics so I took a
Sheena, Queen of the Jungle and a *Hawkman* comic and read
them on the streetcar back.

Ethel had pushed the panic button and called Phil so he was
waiting for me along with Ethel and Pam-Pam in the kitchen.
"Young lady, just where were you?"

"Ethel, didn't you get my note?"

Phil tapped my note that he had put on the table. "In this
family we don't do things like that. What if you had gotten lost?"

"Then I would have called for directions back to your place." I
got a banana out of the bowl and began to peel it. "But I wouldn't
have got lost. I'm used to taking care of myself."

"No doubt you are." Phil drummed his fingers on the tabletop.
"No thanks to that shiftless father of yours."

I stopped peeling the banana and put it down on the table.
"Barney's not shiftless."

"He drove our poor Jeanie to an early grave with all of his
woolly-headed nonsense. We warned her time after time that he
wasn't responsible, but she wouldn't hear anything bad said
about him. And we had to stand by and watch her work herself

to death. She tried to hold down two jobs to pay off his gambling debts, but he lost the money faster than she could earn it."

"Barney's had a tough run of luck is all."

"Barney always had some excuse for being lazy. But he was always irresponsible and he's raising you to be the same way." He reached over the tabletop and drew the comic books to him so that he could read the titles. "Where did you get these?" He began to leaf through them.

"From this neat little place on Market . . ." I would have told them more but Phil the Pill picked up both comics.

"I won't have such trash in my house." And he took the comics and tore them in half. And then he tore them in half again.

"Those were mine!"

He wagged a finger at me. "And you eat my food and you sleep under my roof. And you be grateful, young lady, that not everyone is like your father."

I told myself to keep my temper. It was like Barney always said—though didn't always practice—when it's the house's game, the odds are always stacked against you. I just pushed myself away from the table.

"Where are you going?" he demanded. "I'm not finished talking to you."

"I'm going for a walk. But don't worry. I won't breathe your air."

"But you can't go for a walk, dear." Ethel pointed out the window. "The clouds are blowing in from the sea. It's too cold outside."

"I like to walk in cold, cloudy weather," I said.

Pam-Pam's reaction was typical. Whatever she didn't understand she called crazy. "Who likes cloudy weather?" she asked. "You're weird."

"You can't go out now that it's cloudy. You might catch cold," Phil said. "Now see here, young lady. I won't tolerate any more of your sloppy behavior. I told your mother I'd take care of you."

"And what did Jeanie say back to you?" I asked.

Phil blinked. "What was that?"

"What did my mother tell you after you told her you'd take care of me?"

"Why nothing. She just smiled." He added, "With relief."

"She was smiling because she knew you couldn't take care of a dead cat."

I jerked open the kitchen door and hurried out.

They were the kind of people who liked nothing but sunshiny weather—well, I used to be that way till Barney took me once to look up at the clouds. We hitched our way outside of the city and just looked up at the big sky and Barney made me really look up at the clouds. And sometimes there were spots of silver satin and sometimes there were iron fists and other times there were splotches of silver white where the sunlight was trying to burn its way through the clouds. He made me see that a cloudy day can have more zip to it than a sunny day.

It was unofficially open war after that. If I didn't brush my hair one morning, Phil would drop some casual remark from behind his newspaper that maybe Barney let me keep my hair like a bird's nest but Phil wouldn't allow his daughters to do that, and so he wouldn't let me. And on and on, always badmouthing Barney by criticizing me. And his daughters and even Ethel did the same thing. I gave them all a few days to stop but when school began and Pam-Pam got her friends badmouthing me too, I started hitting back—not literally, even *I* knew better than that. All I had to do was put a little "zip" into their lives, ending with the Saturday that the electric heater warming the water of the birdbath in the backyard went on the blink. I watched the electrician work on it for a little while and then I went into the upstairs john where Pam-Pam was washing up. Pam-Pam, being the youngest and dullest of the family, especially needed some zipping.

I sat down on the bathtub's side watching Pam-Pam brush her teeth. She was always checking her face for new zits, so that her family shouted at her for hogging the john so much. She found extra time to check her face by doing things like dawdling over brushing her teeth, while she checked out her face.

"I bet you could fry the feathers off a couple of birds right now with that electric birdbath."

"That's repulsive," Pam-Pam said.

"You could fry them and serve them right away to your cat. Maybe set up a cat drive-in."

Pam-Pam tried to do what her mother had told her to do, which was to ignore me. She concentrated on brushing her teeth the way nice girls did, with her mouth nearly closed so she didn't spray toothpaste over the mirror. The toothbrush squirmed around behind her lips like a live worm. I told her that.

Pam-Pam tried her best not to think about her toothbrush but concentrate instead on her zits, only it didn't work. Her eyes kept wandering down to her mouth.

"I saw a worm in a rotten apple once. It was crawling just underneath the skin so the skin seemed to move—"

Pam-Pam, toothbrush in hand, went to the doorway, the white foam around her mouth. "Mother. Mother." She stamped one fluffy-slippered foot.

It was almost too easy, really, to get her hysterical. I begged her pardon as I slid on past her. She ignored me and went on shouting. I found my way to the room I shared with the Hedgehog. She was actually very pretty, I suppose, but when I saw her, she usually had her hair up in curlers. I think all that tightening of her hair pulled at the roots too much and maybe loosened her brainstuff inside her skull, because she spent most of her time talking about boys and dresses and dances.

She was rolling her hair when I walked in. She wrinkled up her nose. "What do you think you're doing?"

"I'm wearing a dress like your mother told me to do."

"But she didn't tell you to wear the jeans at the same time."

"It's drafty in a skirt."

The Hedgehog raised her eyebrows and sighed. "What did you do to the brat this time?" Pam-Pam had just stopped yelling in the john.

"I scared her about brushing her teeth." I flopped backwards onto my bed, arms outstretched. "She may never brush her teeth again and they'll all rot and fall out and you'll have to buy her dental plates. And you'll have to get a little motor to raise and lower her plates and there'll be a little whir every time she talks."

"It won't work with me." The Hedgehog picked up one bottle of nail polish and then another before deciding on using a third one.

"What won't work with you?" I asked, disappointed.

"You can't scare me out of the room," the Hedgehog sniffed. "And if you don't watch it, Daddy's going to send you to live with our grandmother because no one else in the family wants such a horrid little child as you."

"I didn't know we had a grandmom." I put my hands behind my head to pillow them. Outside in the hallway I could hear Pam-Pam and her mother talking in quiet but urgent voices.

"You bet we do and as superstitious and impossible to live with as anybody can be." She cocked one eye at me. "You two were just made for each other."

Phil the Pill had come out from his study. He said he was going through his law books, but five will get you two that he was really studying his back issues of *Playboy* or polishing all of his plaques—the biggest of which said he was a former district president of the California Bar Association, a group of lawyers and bartenders. His voice joined Pam-Pam's and his wife's. Finally I heard him say "That does it. She's too much Barney's child and not enough of Jeanie's."

About five minutes later he came into the room. "Would you please excuse us, Annette?"

The Hedgehog got off her bed, throwing me an I-told-you-so smile, and left the room, holding her hand and nails up so the polish already on her nails would not run. Phil looked down at me. He made a point of ignoring the jeans with the dress. "Haven't you been happy here, young lady?"

"It's been a blast, Uncle Phil."

"I'll just bet it has, you little greasy pachuke." Phil stuffed his hands inside his pockets and began rocking up and down on the balls of his feet. "You look so much like Jeanie on the outside that I thought you'd be like Jeanie on the inside, and there never was a sweeter tempered, gentler person than her. But you take after that no-good husband—"

"Careful how you talk about Barney," I said.

Phil the Pill threw back his shoulders and raised his head a little. "I'll talk about him however I like," he said, but I noticed he skipped on over that topic. I'd told Pam-Pam about a week ago that Barney knew a lot of people in San Francisco who owed him favors, so that she'd better not mess around with me. I'd actually told half the truth. Barney knew a lot of people here but he was the one who owed them favors—and money too.

"Anyway, I'm going to send you off to stay with your grandmother. She wanted you to stay with her in the first place when she heard what happened; but out of kindness to you I didn't want you to stay with her."

"You all make her sound like she's the Wicked Witch of the West."

"She's . . . eccentric," Phil the Pill said.

"Meaning she won't let you farm her out to some nursing home."

The muscles worked on the left side of Phil's mouth so I knew I'd hit home. "Get your things together," he said.

We came in by Broadway Street. . . . "Remember now. You call her Paw-Paw."

"What's Paw-Paw?"

"Maternal grandmother. Chinese have a different word for every relation. Like I'm your *kauh-fu*—your maternal uncle. Actually your grandmother's name is *Ah Paw* but when you're close to someone, you repeat the word, so it's Paw-Paw."

"I don't know any Chinese," I said.

Phil grunted. "You don't have to worry about talking to her. She learned pretty good English when she was a maid to some rich Americans."

"When did she do that?"

"Just after your grandfather died. I was only a baby then. But she quit once Jeanie finished high school. She got tired of leaving Chinatown."

He turned the wheel and the car swung down Kearny from Columbus. It was like we'd gone through an invisible wall into another world. There was a different kind of air here, lighter and brighter. I mean, on the north side there were the American bars and topless joints; on the west, the mansions and hotels of Nob Hill; and on the other two sides were the tall skyscrapers where insurance men or lawyers spent the day. And they were pushing all the sunshine and all the buildings of Chinatown together—like someone had taken several square miles of buildings and squeezed it until people and homes were compressed into a tiny little half of a square mile. I didn't know what to make of the buildings either. They were mostly three- or four-story stone buildings but some had fancy balconies, and others had decorations on them like curved tile roofs—one building had bright yellow balconies decorated with shiny, glazed purple dolphins—and there was a jumble of neon signs, dark now in the daytime, jammed all together. Most of the buildings, though, had some color to them—bright reds and rich golds with some green thrown in.

But it was the people there that got me. I don't think I'd ever seen so many Chinese in my life before this. Some were a rich, dark tan while others were as pale as Caucasians. Some were short with round faces and wide, full-lipped mouths and noses squashed flat, and others were tall with thin faces and high cheekbones that made their eyes look like the slits in a mask. Some were dressed in regular American style while others wore padded silk jackets. All of them crowding into one tiny little patch of San Francisco.

Funny, but I felt embarrassed. Up until then I had never thought about skin colors because in the different places where Barney and I had lived, there were just poor people in all different colors. But now all of a sudden I saw all these funny brown people running around, a lot of them gabbling away at one another. I started to roll up the car window to try to shut out the sound and I noticed that my hand on the window handle was colored a honey kind of tan like some of the people outside. I took my hand off the handle and stared at it.

"What's the matter now?" Phil asked. We'd gotten caught in a momentary traffic snarl. I turned to see that Phil's face was brown as my hand. Phil adjusted his tie uneasily and growled, "What're you looking at?"

I looked ahead, keeping my eyes on the glove compartment. Barney and me had never talked much about stuff like this. I knew more about race horses than I knew about myself—I mean myself as a Chinese. I looked at my hands again, thinking they couldn't be my hands, and then I closed my eyes and felt their outline, noticing the tiny fold of flesh at the corners. Maybe it was because I thought of myself as an American and all Americans were supposed to be white like on TV or in books or in movies, but now I felt like some mad scientist had switched bodies on me like in all those monster movies, so that I had woken up in the wrong one.

Suddenly I felt like I was lost. Like I was going on this trip to this place I had always heard about and I was on the only road to that place but the signs kept telling me I was going to some other place. When I looked in the glove compartment to check my maps, I found I'd brought the wrong set of maps. And the road was too narrow to turn around in and there was too much traffic anyway so I just had to keep on going . . . and getting more and more lost. It gave me the creeps so I kept real quiet.

Phil headed up Sacramento Street—a steep, slanting street that just zoomed on and on up to the top of Nob Hill, where the rich people lived and where they had the swanky hotels. Phil turned suddenly into a little dead-end alley wide enough for only one car. On one side was a one-story Chinese school of brick so old or so dirty that the bricks were practically a purple color. On the other side as we drove by was a small parking lot with only six spaces for cars. Phil stopped the car in the middle of the alley and I could see the rest of it was filled with apartment houses. Somewhere someone had a window open and the radio was blaring out "I Want to Hold Your Hand" by that new group, the Beatles. I couldn't find the place where it was coming from but I did see someone's diapers and shirts hung in the windows and on the fire escape of one apartment.

"Why do they hang their laundry in the windows?" I asked Phil.

"That's what people from Hong Kong use for curtains," Phil grumbled.

The sidewalk in front of Paw-Paw's house was cracked like someone had taken a sledgehammer to it, and there were iron grates over the lower windows. The steps up to the doorway were old, worn concrete painted red. To the left were the mailboxes, which had Chinese words for the names or had no labels at all. To the right were the doorbells to all the nine apartments. Phil picked out the last and rang. He jabbed his thumb down rhythmically. Three short. Three long. Three short.

"Why are you doing that?" I asked.

"Signaling your Paw-Paw," he grumbled. "She never answers just one buzz like any normal person, or even just three bursts. It's got to be nine buzzes in that way or she doesn't open the door. She says her friends know what she means."

So did I. It was Morse code for SOS. The buzzer on the door sounded like an angry bee. Phil the Pill opened the door, putting his back against it and fighting against the heavy spring that tried to swing it shut. "Go on. Up three flights. Number nine."

I walked into an old, dim hallway and climbed up the wooden steps. As I turned an angle on the stairs, I saw light burning fierce and bright from a window. When I came to it, I looked out at the roof of the Chinese school next door. Someone had thrown some old 45's and a pair of sneakers down there. If I were some kind of kid that felt sorry for herself, I would almost have said that was the way I felt: like some piece of old, ugly junk that was being kicked around on the discard pile while Barney was getting better.

I didn't stay by the window long, though, because Phil was coming up the stairs and I didn't want to act like his kids' stories about Paw-Paw had scared me. Anybody could be better than Phil the Pill and his family . . . I hoped. I stopped by the number-nine room, afraid to knock. It could not be the right place because I could hear "I Want to Hold Your Hand" coming through the doorway. I scratched my head and checked the numbers on the other doors on the landing. Phil the Pill was still a flight down, huffing and puffing up the steps with my duffel bag—it wasn't that heavy; Phil was just that much out of shape. "Go on. Go on. Knock, you little idiot," he called up the stairwell.

I shrugged. It wasn't any of my business. I knocked at the door. I heard about six bolts and locks being turned. Finally the door swung open and I saw a tiny, pleasant, round-faced woman smiling at me. Her cheeks were a bright red. Her gray hair was all curly and frizzy around her head and a pair of rimless, thick eyeglasses perched on her nose. She was round and plump, wearing a sweater even on a hot day like this, a pair of cotton black slacks, and a pair of open-heeled, flat slippers.

"Paw-Paw?" I asked.

"Hello. Hello." She opened up her arms and gave me a big hug, almost crushing me. It was funny, but even though it was like I said—Barney and me never went in much for that senti-mental stuff like hugging and kissing—I suddenly found myself holding on to her. Underneath all the soft layers of clothing I could feel how hard and tough she was. She patted me on the back three times and then left me for a moment to turn down her radio. It really was her old, white, beat-up radio playing rock music.

"Hey, how about a hand?" Phil puffed as he finally got to the landing.

Paw-Paw shuffled out to the landing in her slippered feet and made shooing motions. "You can go home now. We can do all right by ourselves."

Phil heaved his shoulders up and down in a great sigh and set the bag down. "Now, Momma—"

"Go on home," she said firmly. "We need time by ourselves."

I saw that Phil must have had some fine speech all prepared, probably warning Paw-Paw about me and warning me about in-gratitude. He was not about to give up such an opportunity to make a speech.

"Now, Momma—"

"Go on. You're still not too old for a swat across the backside."

Phil ran his hand back and forth along the railing. "Really, Momma. You oughtn't—"

"Go on," Paw-Paw raised her hand.

Phil gulped. The thought of having a former district president of the lawyers spanked by his own mother must have been too much for him. He turned around and started down the steps. He still had to get in the last word though. "You mind your Paw-Paw, young lady. You hear me?" he shouted over his shoulder.

I waited till I heard the door slam. "Do you know what those buzzes stand for?"

"Do you?" Her eyes crinkled up.

"It stands for SOS. But where did you learn it?"

"When I worked for the American lady, her boy had a toy . . . what do you call it?" She made a tapping motion with her finger.

"Telegraph?"

"Yes. It's a good joke on such a learned man, no?" Her round red face split into a wide grin and then she began to giggle and when she put her hand over her mouth, the giggle turned into a laugh.

I don't think that I had laughed in all that time since Barney's accident a month ago. It was like all the laughter I hadn't been able to use came bubbling up out of some hidden well—burst out of the locks and just came up. Both of us found ourselves slumping on the landing, leaning our heads against the banister, and laughing.

Finally Paw-Paw tilted up her glasses and wiped her eyes. "Philip always did have too much dignity for one person. Ah." She leaned back against the railing on the landing before the stairwell, twisting her head to look at me. "You'll go far," she nodded. "Yes, you will. Your eyebrows are beautifully curved, like silkworms. That means you'll be clever. And your ears are small and close to your head and shaped a certain way. That means you're adventurous and win much honor."

"Really?"

She nodded solemnly. "Didn't you know? The face is the map of the soul." Then she leaned forward and raised her glasses and pointed to the corners of her eyes where there were two small hollows, just shadows, really. "You see those marks under my eyes?"

"Yes." I added after a moment, "Paw-Paw."

"Those marks, they mean I have a temper."

"Oh." I wondered what was to happen next.

She set her glasses back on her nose. "But I will make a deal with you. I can keep my temper under control if you can do the same with your love of adventure and intelligence. You see, people, including me, don't always understand a love of adventure and intelligence. Sometimes we mistake them for troublemaking."

"I'll try." I grinned.

I went and got my bag then and brought it inside Paw-Paw's place and looked around, trying to figure out where I'd put it. Her place wasn't more than ten by fifteen feet and it was crowded with her stuff. Her bed was pushed lengthwise against the wall next to the doorway leading out to the landing. To the right of the door was another doorway, leading to the small little cubicle of a kitchen, and next to that door was her bureau. The wall opposite the bed had her one window leading out to the fire escape and giving a view of the alley, which was so narrow that it looked like we could have shaken hands with the people in the apartment house across from us. Beneath the window was a stack of newspapers for wrapping up the garbage. Next to the window was a table with a bright red-and-orange-flower tablecloth. Paw-Paw pulled aside her chair and her three-legged stool and told me to put my bag under the table. A metal cabinet and stacks of boxes covered the rest of the wall and the next one had hooks from which coats and other stuff in plastic bags hung.

In the right corner of the old bureau were some statues and an old teacup with some dirt in it and a half-burnt incense stick stuck into it. The rest of the top, though, was covered with old photos in little cardboard covers. They filled the bureau top and the mirror too, being stuck into corners of the mirror or actually taped onto the surface.

Next to the photos were the statues. One was about eight inches high in white porcelain of a pretty lady holding a flower and with the most patient, peaceful expression on her face. To her left was a statue of a man with a giant-sized, bald head. And then there were eight little statues, each only about two inches high. "Who are they?" I asked.

"Statues of some holy people," Paw-Paw said reluctantly.

There was something familiar about the last statue on Paw-Paw's bureau. It was of a fat, balding god with large ears, who had little children crawling over his lap and climbing up his shoulders. "Hey," I said. "Is that the happy god?"

Paw-Paw looked puzzled. "He's not the god of happiness."

"But they call him the happy god. See?" I pulled Barney's little plastic charm out of my pocket and pointed to the letters on the back.

Paw-Paw didn't even try to read the lettering. Maybe Barney had already shown it to her long ago. "He's not the god of happiness. He just looks happy. He's the Buddha—the Buddha who will come in the future. He's smiling because everyone will be saved by that time and he can take a vacation. The children are holy people who become like children again."

"What about the others, Paw-Paw?"

"I don't have the words to explain," Paw-Paw said curtly, like the whole thing was embarrassing her.

I sat down by the table on the stool, which was painted white with red flowers. "Sure you do. I think your English is better than mine."

"You don't want to know any of that stuff." With her index finger Paw-Paw rubbed hard against some spot on the tablecloth. "That stuff's only for old people. If I tell you any more, you'll laugh at it like all other young people do." There was bitter hurt and anger in her voice.

I should have left her alone, I guess; but we had been getting close to one another and suddenly I'd found this door between us—a door that wouldn't open. I wasn't so much curious now as I was desperate: I didn't want Paw-Paw shutting me out like that. "I won't laugh, Paw-Paw. Honest."

"That stuff's only for old people who are too stupid to learn American ways," she insisted stubbornly.

"Well, maybe I'm stupid too."

"No." Paw-Paw pressed her lips together tightly; and I saw that no matter how much I pestered her, I wasn't going to get her to tell me any more about the statues on her bureau. We'd been getting along so great before that I was sorry I'd ever started asking questions.

We both sat, each in our own thoughts, until almost apologetically Paw-Paw picked up a deck of cards from the table. "Do you play cards?"

"Some," I said. "Draw poker. Five-card stud. Things like that."

Paw-Paw shuffled the cards expertly. "Poker is for old men who like to sit and think too much. Now I know a game that's for the young and quick."

"What's that?"

"Slapjack." She explained that each of us took half of a deck and stacked it in front without looking at it. Then we would take turns taking the top card off and putting it down in the middle. Whenever a jack appeared, the first one to put her hand over the pile of cards got it. She then mixed the new cards with all the cards she still had in front of her. The first one to get all the cards won the game. It would sound like the advantage was with the person who was putting out the card at that time, but she was supposed to turn up the card away from her so she couldn't see it before the other player.

Paw-Paw had played a lot of card games, since she lived by herself, so she seemed to know when the jacks were going to come up. For a while all you could hear was the *slap-slap-slap*ping of cards and sometimes our hands smacking one another trying to get the pile. And sometimes I'd have more cards and sometimes

Paw-Paw would. Eventually, though, she beat me. She shuffled the deck again. "You're a pretty good player," she grudged.

"Not as good as you, though."

Paw-Paw shuffled the cards, tapping them against the table so the cards in the pack were all even. "We used to play all the time. Your mother, Phil, everyone. We'd hold big contests and make plenty of noise. Only when Phil got older, he only wanted to play the games fancy Americans played like—what's that word for a road that goes over water?"

"A bridge? Phil wanted to play bridge."

"Yes." Paw-Paw put the deck on the table. I wandered over to the bed.

The radio was in a little cabinet built into the headboard of the bed. I lay down on the bed and looked at the radio dial. "Do you like rock music, Paw-Paw?"

"It's fun to listen to," Paw-Paw said, "and besides, *Chinese Hour* is on that station every night."

"*Chinese Hour*?"

"An hour of news and songs all in Chinese." Paw-Paw slipped the cards back carefully into their box. "They used to have some better shows on that station like mystery shows."

"I bet I could find some." I started to reach for the dial.

"Don't lose that station." Paw-Paw seemed afraid suddenly.

"Don't worry, Paw-Paw, I'll be able to get your station back for you." It was playing "Monster Mash" right then. I twisted the dial to the right and the voices and snatches of song slid past and then I turned the dial back to her station, where "Monster Mash" was still playing. "See?"

"As long as you could get it back," Paw-Paw said reluctantly.

I fiddled with the dial some more until I got hold of *Gunsmoke*. It'd gone off the air three years ago but some station was playing reruns. Paw-Paw liked that, especially the deep voice of the marshal. It was good to sit there in the darkening little room, listening to Marshal Dillon inside your head and picturing him as big and tall and striding down the dusty streets of Dodge City. And I got us some other programs too, shows that Paw-Paw had never been able to listen to before.

Don't get the idea that Paw-Paw was stupid. She just didn't understand American machines that well. She lived with them in a kind of truce where she never asked much of them if they wouldn't ask much of her.

"It's getting near eight," Paw-Paw said anxiously. It was only when I got the station back for her that she began to relax. "I was always so worried that I would not be able to get back the station, I never tried to listen to others. Look what I missed."

"But you have me now, Paw-Paw," I said.

"Yes," Paw-Paw smiled briefly, straightening in her chair. "I guess I do."

Chapter Two

I

I LIKED Paw-Paw, but I didn't like my new school in China-town. That Monday Paw-Paw enrolled me into a Catholic gram-mar school because they had an hour of Chinese each day, but she didn't know anything about American schools. The average class was nearly fifty. The nuns who ran the school weren't bad, but they were always making us pray or go to different ceremonies in the chapel. And the playground was only the size of a basketball court, surrounded on all sides by buildings or a giant wooden wall. The boys had one half of the court while the girls had the other; and we were so crowded in that the nuns never let anyone run because they were afraid of someone get-ting hurt.

I could have put up with most of that, but the kids gave me problems. We had to wear these uniforms but Paw-Paw didn't have the money yet to buy material for a blouse and dress or buy a sweater, so I got someone's castoffs in the meantime, in-cluding a sweater that was two sizes too big for me and made me feel like I was walking around in a tent.

On the first day I was standing by myself in the girls' half of the courtyard with my back to a wire mesh fence that kept kids from falling off into the back of an apartment house. Five of the girls from my class stood by the sacristy building where the priest put on his robes. One of them held the bell that the nuns used to call the kids in from recess. They looked over my way and giggled and whispered to one another behind their hands. Finally, I had enough so I walked the ten feet over to them.

"What were you saying?"

The girl with the ponytail leaned over the others and said something in Chinese. The others laughed.

I stepped in front of the girl. "What did you say?"

The girl smiled evilly. "I said . . ." And she repeated the sen-tence in Chinese. The other girls, knowing I didn't understand, all laughed.

"Well, the same to you" was all I could think of saying. I headed past them for the girls' john.

"Rag Bag," the ponytailed girl shouted. The others picked it up.

"Rag Bag."

"Rag Bag."

The girls' john was small but at least the water from the tap looked clear and clean. I splashed it over my face and then got a paper towel and began wiping. That was when I saw myself in the mirror. My skin color and different-shaped eyes were like theirs. Only I didn't want to be like them because they made me feel rotten and fat and ugly. No one had ever made me feel like this when I was in American schools outside of Chinatown. I felt like someone had made a mask out of the features of their face and glued it over my real one so everyone would think I was as stupid and mean as those girls outside . . . those *Chinese* girls.

The worst thing of all was Chinese school. I still get nightmares about it sometimes. I wasn't a bad student in the American school, but one hour out of each day the nuns left several classes and in would come the Chinese teachers. Right away they put me into the dummies' class, which met in an old room used to store old desks that were so old they had little holes with iron bottoms for putting ink bottles into. I found out quick enough that even this class was too tough for me. They taught school on the assumption that the kids already knew some Chinese, so they would explain the simple words in the textbooks with even simpler words—but I didn't even know those simple words.

The teacher was a plain-faced lady whose pancake makeup peeled in little patches so it looked like she had some kind of skin disease. She wore a sleeveless silk dress that hugged her body all the way down to her knees except for the slit that showed one leg.

On Monday the teacher stood in front of the class to read that week's lesson from the thin little paperback that was our textbook. The lesson had a colored picture of ants crawling over a rotten pomegranate and the teacher explained the picture and story with a lot of hand gestures. Then she started to read the story out loud again slowly, accenting each word carefully and pausing after each sentence, which ended in an American-style period. Then she waved at the class to repeat the line. No one else was having trouble reading the words but all I saw was a bunch of squiggly lines so I took out my pencil to copy down the sounds I heard. I did that for about five sentences and then I heard the teacher. "What are you doing?" She spoke as if her mouth were full of marbles when she tried to speak English.

"I'm trying to write down the sounds." I held up my book. "See?"

The teacher's eyebrows came together and she pursed her lips as if she were having trouble following me and wording her own answer. "That no good. You . . . you think too much 'Meri-can. Not think Chinese. Never learn. You erase."

"But how am I going to be able to read the words out loud if I don't know what they sound like?"

I heard the teacher tap her foot impatiently. Even if she had enough English to explain—and I wasn't sure about that—she didn't want to take the time for just one dumb student. I didn't have to know Chinese to see that she ran her class like it was some well-oiled machine. She was so used to a certain routine that she hated to break it. "You erase," she insisted.

"But how—"

"YOU ERASE." She snatched the book out of my hand and hit me with it. She didn't hit me hard enough to hurt, only to shock. Then she tossed my book back on top of my desk. "You 'Merican-born. Lazy. Lazy. Lazy." Then she folded her left arm over her stomach and, holding up her book in her right hand, she began to walk back up the aisle, reading the next sentence in the lesson. I sat for a while, listening to all the crazy sounds, and then I picked up my pencil and slowly began to erase what I had written, leaving the page without any meaning to me.

On Tuesday we had calligraphy where we'd insert a pattern of basic words inside sheets of rice paper and copy the words in ink—it was a bit like painting, so at first I liked it till the teacher slapped my wrist with a ruler for holding the brush wrong and then, because my wrist hurt, I did the words sloppy and got an F.

On Wednesday we got to recite the lesson from memory. The others had no trouble because they at least knew what sounds the words were supposed to be. I memorized as much of the lesson as I was able to get sounds for but even that made the teacher mad because while I think I got the sounds right, I didn't know the tones. Every word in Chinese has a tone—like when your voice rises at the end of a question. I just threw in a tone wherever I wanted, so that at first the teacher winced and finally just hid her face in the textbook and told me to sit down.

Thursday we copied the lesson out on narrow rectangles of rice paper that were ruled off in red ink into squares. You wrote a word in each square—which was pretty easy. But Friday we had to write the lesson out from memory. It was easier for the other kids because it was a story to them, but to me the test meant I had to memorize a pattern of pictures. Still I did okay on that, getting every stroke in the right place. After I'd handed in my test, I sat back in my desk feeling pretty good. The teacher picked up her ballpoint pen and scanned over my test, frowning. Then she got up from her desk and came down the aisle. She clicked her pen shut and threw my test onto my desk. "How you do that? Not one word wrong."

"I learned the lesson," I said.

The teacher's lips moved silently as if she were trying to figure out the words for what she wanted to say next. "This too good. You copy book when I not looking."

"I didn't copy any book," I said indignantly. "I don't cheat."

"You not speak Chinese. You not read. You not even hold brush right. And you do this?" Her voice rose angrily. "You copy book."

"I've got a good memory. Want to see me do it again?"

"You know not enough time. Only five minutes left. You copy book."

"Are you calling me a liar?" I was getting just as mad as she was.

She wanted to go into a real tirade then. The whole class had stopped whatever they were doing, turning to watch us. But she knew that if she did it in Chinese, I wouldn't understand her, so it would be wasted. And yet her English wasn't good enough or she was just too mad to think. All she could say was "You too dumb. You copy book." She said each sound like it was exploding from her mouth. Then she clicked her pen point out and stabbed my test paper and scrawled out a big F across the surface. After that I just gave up trying.

The simplest thing would have been to go to Paw-Paw and ask her to help me, but for one thing I never said I wanted to learn Chinese. I was an American and I couldn't see any good reason to learn a foreign language. And then, too, it hurts your pride when you think you're smart and you have to do things that make you feel dumb.

I couldn't wait for the day when Barney would come and take me out of this nowhere place.

I missed Barney an awful lot then. Even if I had to stay on in this school, I wished he could have been there because Barney had a knack for making me see the good side of things. He'd scrounge around awhile until he could show you how interesting something was—like a cloudy day—or how the person really didn't mean to do that bad thing—like when he got beat up after hitting it big—or how the bad thing would grow into something stronger and better—like the time Moe found a puny little kitten, the runt of the litter. He was going to drown it, but Barney told him how being weak could make someone work at being stronger—like Charles Atlas, the muscle man, or Theodore Roosevelt with his asthma. Well, Moe kept the kitten and even if it didn't develop into the biggest tomcat, it got to be the smartest and so it held its own.

There had to be something good to being Chinese.

I needed Barney's eyes right now. I needed them real bad.

II

MONDAY Paw-Paw wasn't back yet when I got home. Because Paw-Paw never got much from her social-security check, she did piecework in the sewing-machine shops. Piecework meant she got paid for each dress or shirt she completed rather than paid by the hour. If you were good with a sewing machine like Paw-Paw, you could make a little money—provided you worked hard and fast. But Paw-Paw's eyes had been going bad so it took her longer to sew things. In her day Paw-Paw told me she could have outfitted an entire army of American ladies with dresses and provided shirts and trousers for their husbands. At least her hours were flexible.

I dumped my books on the bed and just sat there. I should have started my homework, but all I could think about was getting out of Chinatown.

When the phone rang, I reached up to the little alcove above the bed where Paw-Paw kept the phone and answered it. It was Barney. "Hey, is that you, baby? What are you doing with your Paw-Paw? I called Phil's house and Ethel told me where you'd be."

"Needed a change of scenery, you know." I drew one of my legs up on the bed. "You still in the hospital, Barney?"

"Naw, they finally let me out."

"I can be up on a bus to Stockton this afternoon."

"Don't have to, baby. I'm down here in San Francisco."

"We going to live down here?" I asked, puzzled.

"Got to talk to you about that, baby. You got a paper and pencil?"

I held the receiver between my shoulder and chin and fumbled around, getting out my notebook and a pen. "Yeah. Go ahead."

Barney gave me directions about catching the trolley and made me repeat them. "But Barney," I said when I was finished, "why can't you just come down here?"

"Can you see me using a crutch on a crowded trolley?"

"Okay. It won't take me long to pack."

"No. Don't do that. We gotta talk about that, baby. See you soon."

"All right. See you soon." I wrote a short note for Paw-Paw in big block letters, hoping Paw-Paw might be able to read that kind of writing. Then I caught a big, fat electric trolley that took me straight to the foot of Golden Gate Park. I saw Barney sitting on a bench near the entrance to the park, his crutch beside him. But when I got off the trolley, Barney didn't look very happy to see me. He handed something to a chubby dude who was sitting beside him. The dude got up, stuffing something into his pocket with a satisfied smile, and started walking down the path. With a whine the electric trolley pulled away from the corner rattling and crackling.

"Hey, Barney."

"Sorry, baby," Barney said, disgusted. "I lost your surprise birthday money."

"It won't be my birthday for a while."

"Wanted to give it to you early just in case." I wanted to ask what he meant by that but Barney was going on. "I had a fin off Morey but I got to thinking I could take you out to dinner too so I bet that guy an even number of people would get off the next trolley."

"How many did?"

"You were the fifth one."

"For Chrissake, Barney, why didn't you tell me? Then I'd have gotten off at the next stop."

"I just had this feeling all of a sudden." Barney shrugged. "How was I to know you'd be on it?" He grabbed hold of his crutch and got up. "Come on. I can at least take you around the fuchsia gardens. They can't take that from me."

That was only because Barney hadn't found a way of betting his eyeballs yet, but I didn't say that. "I'd rather have you around than any money. But why can't I go with you now?"

Leaning on his old, beat-up crutch, Barney limped along under the tall eucalyptus trees with the skinny, pointed needles. He kicked a big fat pinecone out of his way. And far away I could hear some old Italians shouting excitedly as they played bocce ball. "That's what I come down to tell you, baby. It's gonna take a little longer than I thought at first."

"But you're walking again."

We topped the rise and Barney just stared down at the pebbled, sloping path. I didn't say anything. I just took his arm. Together we hobbled down to the two-lane street and when the cars had all gone by on either side, we crossed the road and went down into the little valley where the fuchsia plants were. The big fat bushes were covered with little bell-like flowers of every color you could think of—from white blossoms with red insides to red-and-purple flowers with every delicate shade in between. We took a small dirt path that twisted into a regular pebbled road and followed that to where there were some benches off the side of the path. The moment we sat down, a squirrel started to creep belly-down closer and closer to us, nose wriggling. Then it stood up, paws held before its white velvety chest as it begged.

I searched around in my sweat-shirt pockets, but I didn't have any cookie or cracker crumbs. And I didn't have a nickel to go back to the peanut vendor to buy one of his bags. To ride the trolley, I used my trolley ticket that gave you ten rides for fifty cents.

"Christ," Barney said through clenched teeth. "Oh, Christ." And he folded his hands over his nose and with his thumb and fingers pinched the corners of his eyes. And I could see the tears coming down. "I haven't even got a nickel to give you, baby."

"He'll be just as happy with this," I said. I picked up a nut that lay near my foot and chucked it over lightly so that it rolled to the feet of the squirrel. It bent over and sniffed at the nut, forepaws dangling limply before it. Then it straightened, wriggling its nose and holding its forepaws up like it wanted to punch me.

I brought my fingers up near my nose and smelled the menthol on them. The nut must have been one of those eucalyptus nuts I'd heard about in school. The squirrel started nosing the ground away from us. "Who cares about a stupid old squirrel anyway," I muttered.

"Oh, God, baby, if only I'd waited till we were back together." Barney drew the back of one arm across his eyes.

"Barney, you didn't start gambling already?"

"The hospital bills were so big, baby, that I got scared. And since my luck has turned, you know, I thought it'd be okay." Barney stumped the ground with his crutch. "I really didn't think I'd get in that deep, baby. We were so close to a penthouse that other time. I was actually dreaming about lying in a penthouse that night I got robbed." Now that he'd tasted big money, I guess he'd gotten even more reckless than before.

"How much are you into Big Mike for?"

"A thousand."

"Already?" But I knew how easy it was for Barney to get into that kind of trouble, especially when he knew I wouldn't be waiting up for him when he got finished. Knowing he'd have to answer to me as soon as he got finished with one of his gambling sessions or poker games usually kept him cautious. I'd never let him get that deep in the hole.

" 'Fraid so," Barney said. "And Big Mike won't take my word for it that I'll pay him off. He says I gotta pay a couple of hundred on account real quick. He's not gonna let me pay him back just twenty bucks a week or anything like that. That means I gotta travel light and fast so it's going to take a little longer for us to get together than I figured at first."

"You promised me this was only temporary. Are you trying to ditch me?"

"Oh, no, baby. Nothing like that." Barney put his arm around me. "You know I can't do without you. It's just that I got it all figured out. I'll keep moving around and won't try to push my luck like last time. If my luck don't start working at small stakes, I'll just move on to another town and another game. And let's say my luck takes a little longer to get working again—say till the summer. Well, you'll be out of school by then and we can go around picking fruit like we usually do. You know, apricots and cherries, apples, tomatoes. That junk. And with you watching the budget, we'll have the money I need in no time to keep Big Mike off my back."

I wriggled out of Barney's arm. "But summer's ten months off. Why can't I go with you now? I can travel light."

Barney pressed his lips together and shook his head. "It don't work that way, baby. You can't go to school one day and then disappear the next. Otherwise the social worker comes sniffing around. They could take you away from me. They could even put you in a foster home. That's why I've always been careful about when we moved."

"I'd like to see them try to put me away," I said. But I never could bluff Barney either at cards or at something like this. "Well, look. Why don't I go with you to, well, like Fresno. I could stay put. Work some angles. Maybe even come up with the money you need."

"You can't stay by yourself for one or two months and that'd be how long I'd have to be dodging around."

I also realized then that Barney would be easier for Big Mike to find if Barney had me in tow—only Barney didn't want to tell me that. "Big Mike's got some nerve muscling you this way after he let you get robbed outside his place," I said bitterly. "I gotta good mind to turn him in. Maybe he had some of his goons rob you himself."

"Big Mike'll do a lot of things, but he pays up when it's due." Barney added with a sad laugh, "It's too bad he expects everyone else to do the same."

I sagged further down on the bench till my head rested against the bench. I wanted out of Chinatown real bad; but I knew Barney was in bad trouble and having me with him would have just made more trouble for him. "Well, it's just as well," I said. I didn't want to add to Barney's worries. "I mean it's such a blast in Chinatown, you know?"

Barney seemed to perk up. "Got plenty of friends?"

"Sure. Sure."

Barney smiled, looking a little more relaxed. "Guess it'd be hard for you to leave then."

"Yeah, sure." I tried to balance the heel of my right foot on the toe of my left. "Why'd you meet me out here? You staying near the park?"

"No, but my ride was stopping near here so I thought you might like to see it. This used to be your mom's favorite place."

"No kidding?" I asked. Barney never liked to talk much about Jeanie, my mom. The few times I asked him about her he'd gotten real uptight about it. And at first I hadn't understood but the last time I asked him, he explained it hurt him too much to talk about her. So I knew what this moment really cost him now to share this memory with me.

Barney nodded around. "That's right. We used to catch the bus out here when we were kids. She always saved part of her lunch to feed the squirrels. Our folks didn't have much money and so once all she had was a lettuce sandwich."

"Was that all?"

"Oh, it had some ketchup. The squirrels loved it anyway."

I looked around the little valley at the tall eucalyptus trees that soared upwards all around the bushes. The light seemed to filter through their branches, hanging in clumps just like their leaves. It was restful here and far away I could hear the sound of calliope music that Barney said came from the carousel over in the children's playground.

Barney reached behind us and pulled lightly at one branch, drawing it over the back of the bench and down so I could see the blossoms better. It was like someone had stuck a bell of one color inside a larger bell. The outer bell on this one was a vermillion red while the inner bell was a deep lavender color. "She liked these the best."

I started to reach my hand up to pluck one, but Barney let go of the branch so that it snapped back behind the bush with a loud rustling sound. "Jeanie never picked them. She always said to let them grow. They'll know when it's time to let go." Barney leaned over the side of the bench, fishing around in the dirt behind it. He lifted up a blossom and dusted the dirt from it lightly and then he held it on his palm. "You see. It's still near perfect condition."

I took the blossom from his palm, holding it in the cup of my hand so I could sniff its delicate scent. "This is the best birthday present I've ever had. Thanks, Barney."

"You're not mad about the money?" Barney seemed surprised.

I wrapped the blossom carefully in a Kleenex so I could press it in a book when I got home. "You can't buy anything like this with money."

"Yeah." Barney scratched his cheek doubtfully. "I guess."

"No, honest," I said. "You know my cousin Pamela? Well, she hardly ever sees her father. I was there on her birthday and Phil didn't get home from this golf game he had with these big-shot politician friends of his till after she'd blown out the candles on her cake and opened up her presents."

"Poor kid," Barney agreed.

I stowed the flower away inside my sweat-shirt pocket. It was getting kind of chilly so I pulled the sweat-shirt hood up over my head. "And I understand about your not being able to take me with you."

"It's only temporary, baby. Like I told you."

"Sure, Barney. But you'll write me when you can?"

"Oh, sure, sure, baby. And call you up too. Now that my luck's really turned, we'll be back together in no time and Big Mike will be crying into his beer."

While he was telling the story about what we'd do when he hit it big, I slipped his good-luck charm into his pocket without him noticing. I figured he needed it more than me. When he was finished telling the story, I got up. "Take me for a walk around the gardens, Barney. Just like you used to do with Jeanie, okay?"

Barney shrugged. "If that's what you really want, baby. Sure."

III

I LEFT Barney hitching his way out of the city, leaning on his crutch and thumbing with his free hand. Paw-Paw didn't get back until long after I did. She'd been sewing some extra shirts for a rush order. When I came out of the kitchen with our tea, I found Paw-Paw sitting back in her chair, her rimless glasses perched on the table like some strange insect, while she rubbed at her eyes.

"Does your head hurt again, Paw-Paw?"

"A little," she admitted. She took her hands down and I could see the red spot on each side of her nose, made by the nose pads of the glasses.

"I saw Barney today," I said.

"Oh?" Paw-Paw stiffened ever so slightly. She put her glasses on. "What did he say?"

"Oh, he's got this deal." I tried to shrug casually. "It's not all that big but it could lead to other things so he's got to follow it up. Mind if I stay for a little while longer?"

I'm not sure, but Paw-Paw looked a little relieved. She picked up one of her decks of cards. "Well, if you're going to stay, you might as well earn your keep by playing slap-jack. You deal first." She slapped the deck of cards down in front of me with a smile.

In the days that followed, I'd get these postcards from Barney. Sometimes they'd be the kind that you bought in the bus depot—like a scenic view of the Milpitas garbage dump—or like the kind you find in a cheap hotel with a view of the hotel thirty years ago when the carpets were new and there weren't any winos sitting outside in front of the windows.

On the back of each postcard, there'd be more or less the same message. Barney hoped I was getting along okay and he was doing fine—Barney was never much one for writing. I mean, if he could have just sent a one-page letter saying he missed me—or something—but he never did. That was never part of Barney's style, and he was never in one place long enough for any of my letters to reach him. The couple of times I tried to write, I got the letters back marked *ADDRESSEE MOVED, NO FORWARDING ADDRESS*. He never tried calling, because I guess he didn't have much money.

And in all that time I just couldn't get used to Chinatown. In the mornings, I would wake up in the cool, crisp air to the voices in the narrow alley rising louder and higher in that strange, musical language. And there would already be the smell and sound of meat and noodles and vegetables frying in hot oil. I would walk the high-slanting streets that seemed to be slipping off the lap of the land into the bay and hear the clack of Mah-Jong tiles or the whine of someone's moon guitar, and I would feel different from everyone else—like somebody jammed into a stranger's body. I felt trapped—like Barney was never going to come for me and I would never be able to get beyond those invisible walls around Chinatown again—I would always be on exhibit in the zoo for all the tourists to gawk at.

One Saturday morning, I woke up shivering and the springs creaked as Paw-Paw leaned over me. "Are you cold, girl?"

"No," I said.

She sat there for a moment and then said, "Well, I am." She got off the bed we shared, sitting on the edge for a moment while she felt with her feet for her heelless slippers. The slippers made her walk a little funny. She would take a very short step, bringing her foot down so that the slipper slapped against her heel, and she would finish the rest of the step with a short shuffle and then lift her other foot and do the same thing with it. When she walked into the kitchen, it was with quick slapping and whispering noises.

I heard her light one of the gas jets on top of the stove and then heard water running into one of her deep enamel pots, making a high, thin drumming sound. She grunted as she planted that on the stove. Then she shuffled back in, taking her winter coat off the hanger that hung by the hook on the edge of the closet, and draped that over me.

"Really, Paw-Paw, I'm fine."

She smoothed the hair back from my head. Despite all the lotion she put on her palms, they still felt like soft, well-oiled leather. "Ah, I forget that children today are tougher than I was at their age. You could bite your way through steel chains, couldn't you?"

"Course, I could." I watched how my breath steamed in the light coming from the one streetlight in the alley, soft and full in the square of the window. Paw-Paw got up to shrug awkwardly into the bright bathrobe of hers. When I first saw it, I thought I had never seen anything in worse taste in my life—I mean turquoise and emerald flowers on yellow cloth—but Paw-Paw even seemed proud of it. I suppose she went by some other kinds of taste—maybe my tastes seemed even a little drab to her. I think she had made the robe for herself from cloth she had bought. At any rate she shuffled across the floor to the table and took out a Winston. She lit the cigarette in one flaring motion of the match. She shifted on the chair so that the street-light fell full on the table and she took out an old, worn deck of cards and began to play. And the cards made soft slapping sounds like dozens of little people in Chinese slippers.

I don't know why, but I began to cry, softly at first, the tears just slipping out of my eyes no matter how hard I tried to close them, and then because it got harder to breathe, I began to sob. I tried to hide my face in my pillow to stop the sounds, but I couldn't. Paw-Paw had the sense to leave me alone for a moment and not touch me. "What's wrong, girl?"

It wasn't just one thing that got to me: not just the small room, or the pawnshop look to the place, or the tiny kitchen, or the way we had to eat in this crummy little room, or the toilet that we had to share with the rest of the floor. There wasn't any door or anything and you took your own toilet paper in with you. And it wasn't the dark hallways, and the junk piled outside each apartment on the landing. And it wasn't washing out our clothes in a small blue basin in the kitchen sink each night. And it wasn't the cockroaches—no matter how much Paw-Paw sprayed and how much she cleaned up, they always kept coming back. No, it was just a whole bunch of things that I couldn't name.

"What's wrong, girl?" Paw-Paw asked. "Your stomach, does it hurt?"

"I'll be all right in just a moment," I said, but the more I tried to hold back the tears, the more I cried. Paw-Paw got up from her chair and shuffled over to the bed. She put her arm around me clumsily and patted me lightly on the back.

"It's all right to cry. You cry and you wash your heart clean." And suddenly it felt like the most natural thing to fit myself against Paw-Paw and cry on her shoulder and feel how the rough cloth of her robe drank up my tears.

After a while I sat back up and began to wipe my eyes on the back of my sleeve.

"Hey, girl. Your eyes will only get redder that way. Use some Kleenex." And she pulled several tissues from the box on the headboard and handed them to me.

"I don't know what got into me." When I was finished wiping my eyes, I balled the tissues up in my fist.

"Did you feel that you were all alone inside?" Paw-Paw asked.

I looked at her in amazement. "How did you know?"

"All of our family go through that. I did. Your mother did too. We're all children of the Owl Spirit, you see?" Paw-Paw opened up the neck of her pajamas and took out a little jade charm hanging from a golden chain. I touched it, feeling the warmth of her body. "Jade is a living stone. The more you wear jade," she told me proudly, "the greener it gets." The jade was a deep, warm green—like the green of a tree leaf when you hold it up against the sun.

Up to then, I had thought of Chinese art as a bunch of vases and snuff bottles with a lot of gentlemen and ladies sitting in a garden drinking tea; and if they were really whooping it up, they'd even be smiling. But the charm looked more like Mexican Indian stuff. It was like someone had taken a full, frontal view of an owl and slit it down the middle and spread the parts out across the charm. And every little part had come to life and was playing a violent game with the other parts: an eyebrow was more than an eyebrow, it was also a little scaled dragon that was trying to swallow up the eyes which weren't just eyeballs— they were also miniature snakes swallowing their own bodies before the dragon could get them. But it was the smiling beak that caught my attention—it seemed at any moment ready to crawl off the charm and down over my arm. The smiling beak, sinuous and twisting, was a tiger, dangerously playful as it stretched its paws and tail ever so slightly upwards across the broad feathered cheeks (that also looked like fields of what I thought was grain but which Paw-Paw said were rice plants) toward the snake eyeballs.

"Can you tell what the charm is a picture of?"

I blinked my eyes and tried to see the whole design. "It's an owl . . . I think."

"Yes," Paw-Paw smiled, pleased.

"It must be very valuable." I let it go gently so it dropped back lightly against Paw-Paw.

"Some things you can't count in coins. The Owl Spirit gave it to our family." She paused and I had the feeling that she was lost somewhere inside herself, groping for the right words. "American owls may be good and wise but Chinese owls are supposed to be evil—though most Chinese don't know that anymore. Even many of the old ones have forgotten, as they have forgotten many things. Those Chinese owls, many have no sense of family. Many make fun of their parents and when the parents grow too old, the young owls push them out of the nest. Some even eat their poor old parents. And they steal people's souls."

Paw-Paw settled back against the headboard and puffed at her cigarette. "Now the story happened a long, long time ago when our ancestors first came into southern China—when the hills and valleys were covered by the same jungle that had been put there when the world was first made. And that jungle, it was like a dark-green sea flooding over the hills and pouring into the valleys with only a hole here and there in the vast surface to let someone go in. But when I was a girl back in China, there was nothing left of that jungle except maybe when I was walking through the orchards or the rice paddies, I'd hear this far, faraway sound of leaves rustling and wild animals coughing and growling. In those early days, there were only a few soldiers, and their families, sent down to guard the mines and trade routes; they fed themselves by what they could grow or kill."

And then Paw-Paw began her story, which went more or less like this:

The two owls, Jasmine and Peony, sat up high in their favorite sighting tree where they could see over the wall surrounding the village of the walkers. Since the large, odd walkers had blundered into this part of Jasmine and Peony's jungle, the walkers had given the two owls much amusement, and the owls looked upon the walkers with the same proprietary air they had once reserved for the tender little munchables that had always been their prey.

Peony coughed up a small pellet of fur and bone, spitting it outward so that it disappeared somewhere in the dense tangle of branches below. "I think the walkers must really be some kind of ape because they have the same strange, soft, wormlike talons." Peony balanced on one foot and tried to flex the talons of her other foot to illustrate her point. "And they make up for not having any tails or much hair by wearing all those funny, bright-colored skins that they can take off and put on."

"No," Jasmine, her sister, insisted. "They're more like pigs because they root about in the dirt all the time."

"But look at them." Peony nodded her head at the village. "Only apes try to walk around on their hind legs." The owls' eyes were so sensitive that they could see the very souls of the walkers beginning to leave the little artificial caves that they liked to build. (When we sleep, you see, one of our two souls leaves the body to go wandering, and what it sees makes up our dreams.) Some of the dream-souls soared high into the air, journeying to far places. But many of the dream-souls walked through the village gates to work in the fields that the walkers had cleared from the jungle and flooded with water so they could grow their grasslike plants. The dream-souls worked in the fields at night just as their bodies did in the daytime. By this the owls knew the walkers were worried, for this year the rains had not come from the sea as they usually did and there was less water in the fields and fewer munchables to be found in the jungle. That is why so many of Jasmine's brothers and sisters floated silently in the open air above the sparkling, moonlit fields, hunting the little animals that were drawn to the plants.

"Mother's finally got something," Jasmine said. Huffing and puffing, their mother rose to join them in their tree with awkward flutterings of her wings. Gripped in her talons was a small mouse. But as she was about to light on their branch, a shape appeared suddenly. Their mother dropped her wings low to protect her catch and there was a solid thump as she went tumbling through the air. One of their brothers hovered above them, hooting at the trick he had played.

"How dare—" their mother began indignantly when one of their older sisters suddenly soared upward from below and snatched the mouse from her. Their mother's talons clutched at the air feebly as if she could not believe they were now empty.

"This place is for hunters, not for ducks," their brother said contemptuously. "You flap your wings so loud you scare the munchables away."

"Well," said their sister, "if one of you quacks like a duck, perhaps I'll throw it to you. Or waddle. Yes, go ahead and waddle."

"If I were a hundred years younger, you wouldn't dare say that," protested their mother. She was among the most ancient of owls, so old that it was said she had seen the dew rise in ghostly streamers of steam when the sunlight touched the jungle on the first day after the making of the world. For a long time their mother had been one of the most powerful owls, but in the last few centuries, she had started to forget many things and had lost some of her magical abilities. Worse yet, in the opinion of the other owls, she had become almost unnaturally sentimental.

Jasmine and Peony were the only two who had survived her last hatching over a thousand years ago, and their mother had spoiled them terribly, so that they were as slavish and mindless as ducks. Though Jasmine and Peony were each old enough to live by herself as a proper owl would have done, they insisted on staying in the same tree with their mother and doing everything together.

Even through the hardest times, Jasmine and Peony had refused to leave her, though it had become obvious when they had been growing up that their mother could do little to protect them from the rest of their family. While Jasmine and Peony had still been small, their aging mother had been ruthlessly forced away from one hunting territory after another, sometimes by a son, sometimes by a daughter. It had been fortunate for Jasmine, Peony, and their mother that the walkers had come stumping into this part of the jungle to clear the land and grow their funny grasslike plants. In fact, the plants had drawn so many sweet little munchables that they had shared the fields with the rest of their family without much argument—until now.

Jasmine lowered her head and spread her tail and wings so that she looked twice as large and dangerous. Then, eyes glaring and head bobbing up and down, she snapped her beak angrily. "Come, see if I have a duck's bite or duck's feet, brother dear."

Peony also lowered her head. "Yes, come see, sister dear."

Their older brother and sister hesitated, for Jasmine and Peony were now old enough and strong enough to be formidable foes. And their mother took advantage of the moment to sweep in with some of her old grace and snatch back her mouse, dealing a buffet with her wings to the heads of both her son and daughter. Then she landed on the branch beside her two younger daughters, giving a little hop of triumph.

"*Pah.*" Their brother spat out a pellet. "I've better things to do with my time." And he drifted away in a leisurely circle back toward the fields. Their sister floated away with him.

"What's that wailing?" Jasmine asked.

"It must be some family of walkers," their mother said indifferently. "They always carry on that way when one of them dies."

And sure enough, from one of the artificial caves still brightly lit slipped two souls, each exactly like the other. After walking mournfully about the village and then the fields, the dream-soul began the long trek across the dikes, heading toward the Yellow Springs, the kingdom of the dead, while the other stayed to haunt the grave site as a ghost.

"I'm glad it isn't our walkers," Jasmine said.

"No, see, there they go now," Peony said. She nodded her head at five dream-souls that walked across the dikes. The father limped as if with an old war wound and behind him came the mother and three sons. Four of them began working in the fields where Jasmine, Peony, and their mother liked to hunt. The dream-souls weeded their fields diligently and tended their plants so conscientiously that they were the largest and sweetest in the area, drawing many tender munchables across the dikes that bordered each field. But the dream-soul of the third son, the youngest of the walkers, crashed on into the jungle, armed with his funny flying claws, as the owls called them. Each claw was a sharp little metal triangle that he fastened to a stick with feathers at the bottom. He had another much larger stick with a string attached from one end to the other. He would take one of his flying claws and, putting the feathered end against the string, draw back on the string so that the big stick bent in the middle and the metal triangle of the little stick would almost touch the middle of the big stick. When he let go of the string of the big stick, the little stick would fly hissing through the air.

"We haven't helped out the young walker in his hunting in a long time," Peony reminded them guiltily. They had found the young walker vaguely comical as he blundered on through the jungle—though he was much better at it than most walkers—trying to pretend he was some great hunter, like an owl or a tiger. And in the past, Jasmine and Peony, sticking to the shadier parts of the jungle, would scare some game to where even the poor-sighted, clumsy walker could kill it, which was their way of repaying the family of walkers for the hunting grounds the walkers had given them: presenting the walkers the game in the same spirit that the lady of a huge manor might toss a few pennies at festival time to the people who tended her fields.

"Oh, why bother ourselves about them?" grumbled their mother. She fluffed the downy feathers on her chest. "There will always be some walkers to take their places in the fields."

But the drought went on until the walkers' plants withered in the now dry, stone-hard fields. More and more of the walkers died until the graveyard was filled with mournful—sometimes even spiteful—ghosts. And there came a time when the young walker saw his mother trying to boil withered grass—real grass this time—and he had shaken his head. "We're not cattle." And he had gone deep into the jungle, determined to fetch back something, but though he heard many animals, he never saw any and so he walked further and further into a part where there were strange tall trees, their trunks branded with diamond patterns and their branches and leaves beginning only at their tops, looking like huge green feathers. Giant ferns stirred around his legs and waist like green mist. The young walker went so far that night fell before he could find his way out.

Voices rose about him in the darkness, the voices of tiny things sounding no less dangerous than the voices of the large. After walking a little, the young walker found himself in a clearing of strange trees, their trunks and branches twisting in every direction. Since part of their roots grew above ground, the trees looked as if they were struggling free of the ground to dance about in a frenzy. As afraid as he was of the trees, the young walker preferred them to the dangers of the ground so he climbed up one hurriedly, where eventually, despite all his fears, he fell asleep.

Not far away was Jasmine's tree. Now all of the owls had become thin and bony during the drought and more than one of Jasmine's brothers and sisters had cast an eye on their mother, but had held off suggesting they make a meal of her out of respect for Jasmine's and Peony's talons and beaks. But as their stomachs began to shrivel and their talons found less and less game, the more attractive their weak mother seemed. Until finally all the brothers and sisters banded together before their mother grew any thinner. Jasmine and Peony fought as best they could and though they were outnumbered, they managed to hold off the others until their mother escaped into the jungle. Then they followed her, finding her several hours later.

In the meantime, the young walker sat restlessly in his tree, the noise of the owls' fighting having drawn his wandering dream-soul back to his body, so that he had awakened. He looked across the clearing and in the moonlight saw on the limb of the tree across from him three owls, round of body and of head with solemn eyes and small tufted ears. The one in the middle was larger and looked older than the other two, but the feathers of all three were torn and bedraggled and there were cuts on all of them, as if they had just been in some fierce battle and were now too worn out to be on their guard.

There wasn't much meat to them, the young walker thought, but at least there would be something for the pot. As he had been taught by his father, he raised his bow and arrow quietly as he drew in his breath and released the arrow when he let his breath out. The string twanged loudly in the air and the arrow flew, the metal head glittering silver under the moon. It pinned the middle owl to the trunk of the tree. Its claws skittered and scrabbled at the branch as it tried to regain its clawhold and then it fell still, hanging dead on the arrow.

The other two owls rose from the branch, circling the tree and making startled cries that sounded like "Mother! Mother!"

The young walker was so surprised that he simply sat in his tree, forgetting to kill the other two owls. They flew round and round the tree crying until suddenly one of them stopped, hovering in the air. It turned its wide-circled eyes on him—eyes where the feathers spread outwards like petals, as if the eyes were the centers of shimmering, night-growing flowers. And in a panic, the young man slid down the trunk of the tree, ignoring cuts and bruises, finally losing his grip, and falling with a crash into the bushes. He scrambled out of them, forgetting his bow and arrow, and ran through the forest. If he tripped on a root and fell, he went on crawling forward until he could get to his feet again, for he was afraid to stop for one moment.

But it seemed to him as he fled that the flowerlike eyes followed him. He ran until his legs gave out and his lungs ached, so that every breath felt like the air was on fire. He knew then that he could not escape the forest that night and so he climbed up another tree, where finally in fits and snatches he fell asleep again from sheer exhaustion.

And as he slept, his dream-soul slipped loose from his body and on the branch above saw Jasmine and Peony, who had taken the forms of fair young walkers, as was in their power, for it was easier to make themselves understood this way. Their faces were lovely and yet strange and willful at the same time and their lips pushed slightly outwards as if pouting, or like beaks. Both were dressed in long, flowing gowns of large feathers. Their hair was white, flecked with brown and coiled in heavy braids about their heads like helmets, except for the top where the tips of two braids rose in little tufts. And they called the soul of the walker underneath the branch where they sat, their legs dangling.

"Did we save our mother from being eaten by our family so some grass-eater like you could kill her?" Jasmine angrily accused him.

And the young walker spoke carefully. "I did not know. My own parents are starving."

And Jasmine was filled with a mindless rage such as she had never felt, for added to her grief was the fact that her mother had been killed by some grass-eating walker. It was an insult to the very order of the world, which said that owls were the hunters, and grass-eaters like munchables and walkers were put their for their pleasure. "You do not know what hunger really is, but you will." Jasmine smiled and her smile was more terrifying than her laugh, for her laugh had simply been frightening, but her smile was terrible and yet beautiful at the same time. As terrible and beautiful as the deadly, flowing motion of a tiger. And then Jasmine leapt from the branch and Peony with her, leaving the soul of the young walker alone, listening to the weird laughter drifting back to it through the dark trees.

Jasmine's brothers and sisters were as angry as she and Peony when they heard of their mother's death—not so much because their mother had been killed but because a walker had dared strike down one of the feathered folk. From that time on, no matter how far the young walker traveled during the day, he could kill nothing, even though, unlike the other hunters, he found an animal every day. Sometimes it would be a deer with fat haunches, or a rabbit still plump despite the drought; but whatever it was, just as he would begin to draw back his bowstring, Jasmine or one of her family would hoot and the animal would flee and then the owl would laugh mockingly at the young walker. The other hunters would occasionally bring back sparrows or squirrels or at least something out of which to make a broth, but each day the young walker would come back with nothing.

And Jasmine watched with growing satisfaction as piece by piece the young walker's family sold all the furniture in their house and then their precious farming tools and finally even their house and land—which was perhaps the hardest of all for the walkers to bear because next year, though they would work the land that they themselves had cleared, most of the crop would go to the new owner.

But the gods had no pity and the next year the rains still did not come from the sea. And the young walker still had no luck hunting. The mother and father walkers grew so thin that the owls could count their ribs and see the knobby joints of their elbows and knees. The oldest of the three brothers could not stand to see such a thing happen so he sold himself into slavery before he was too weak to fetch a good price. And the owls watched in scornful delight as the slaver led the brother away, while the rest of the walkers wept and cried out as disgustingly as ducks. And with the money the oldest son fetched, the family was able to buy rice that lasted them for a year because they only took one mouthful each day. And on occasion, in the deep of the night, one of Jasmine's family would fly over the house and laugh mockingly and shout in the language of the walkers, "Dig, dig, dig your graves!"

In time, though, Jasmine tired of the sport. She declared herself satisfied but her family was not, for the game was even more pleasurable than swooping down on some helpless little animal. So the third year, when the rains still would not come from the sea and the famine went on, Jasmine's family continued driving the game away from the young walker.

The second brother saw their mother and father lying pitifully on their rush mats, for they had grown even thinner than before and were now too weak to even move. There was not even enough strength in their bodies to heal the sores that began appearing on their skins. He and his brother were far too thin and weak themselves to fetch a good price as slaves but he remembered some of the old stories of what some sons had done for their parents out of love. He fell to his knees, weeping. "Father and Mother, you gave me the flesh of my body once. Let me give some of it back to you."

And so saying, he went to the hearth and with a knife he cut strips of flesh from his legs and peeled them off to drop into a kettle of boiling water, making a life-giving broth which he served to them; and the broth was so magical that his parents and himself and his brother did not have to eat for a month.

And Jasmine, when she saw the walker, realized what he was doing and felt sorry for him. "Surely everything is balanced now."

"Have you forgotten Mother?" Peony asked her.

"Have you forgotten all the owls?" one of Jasmine's brothers argued. "Do you want the walkers to think they do anything they like within our jungle?"

And as the drought continued, month by month, the second son cut a little more from himself until there was nothing to give; for he was nothing but a thin covering of bloody skin over bones. So finally he climbed into the kettle himself.

He sat quietly till the water began to bubble around him and then calmly he began stirring the water about him with a long spoon. He was so thin and light now that he began to turn round and round in the water as he stirred. And when the flesh fell of his bones, the skeletal arm and hand still held the spoon and went on stirring. And for the rest of the night, the family could hear the clanking of the spoon and the bones against the side of the kettle. But finally even the bony arm fell apart.

Jasmine's family had been sitting upon the wall of the village, knowing that the middle son must die. They had ignored all the other souls of the dead walkers that had tiptoed past the owls on their way to the land of the dead. The two souls of the second son tried to crawl down the street, staying as much as they could in the shadows, but Peony's eyes were too sharp. She sprang from the wall, snatching up both souls in her talons and holding them flapping and tugging and shrieking to be let free, while a brother forced the souls inside an empty gourd he held. When the souls were inside, he plugged the mouth with a stopper he had in his beak. And upon the wall Jasmine's brothers and sisters hopped about, their talons clacking, and joined with Peony in hooting laughingly.

Realizing what had happened, the young walker looked out the door to see Jasmine and her family on the wall. Peony laughed at the young walker and shook the small gourd at him mockingly so that the souls trapped inside wailed. And the wailing set Peony and the others off into a fresh round of laughter. Only Jasmine was silent.

The young walker fell to his knees and bowed his head till his forehead touched the dirt. "Let his souls find release and you may do what you want with me," begged the young walker. "Punish me but not my family."

And the owls, except for Jasmine, mocked the young walker for being so duckishly attached to another brother and dared him to fetch back his brother's souls.

Jasmine twisted her head around to Peony. "Sister, let him have the souls. He is doing no more than what you or I would do for one another."

"When we're finished with them," Peony snapped, "and not before." And she leapt up from the wall, the gourd still held in her talons, and her brothers and sisters followed her into the jungle and Jasmine last of all, twisting her head around as she flew away to look back at the young walker, who still knelt in the dirt.

When the owls disappeared into the jungle, the young walker rose, dusting off his knees, and went back inside the house. He took a sip of the broth and, leaving the kettle of broth for them, said good-bye to his mother and father, for he swore he would not return until he had set his brother's souls free.

The young walker never saw the owls, only heard them laughing in the night as they played with his brother's souls. He slept by day and followed them at night, through all the tiger and wolf spirits and the ghosts and all the other creatures of the darkness and the shadow. And he followed the owls for days and days until he came to a small clearing one evening.

Jasmine and her family had taken the form of walkers, the better to mock the souls of the walker by dancing and singing as the walkers did at one of their festivals. And because the night was hot, they had taken off their feather dresses and robes while they danced. Jasmine did not dance, having no heart for such a thing, but she sang at Peony's request because she had the finest voice of the family.

The dance her family danced was a rather owlish one. At the start of each stanza, they bowed formally to one another; and then, nodding their heads, they turned slowly with arms outspread to catch wind and moonlight, gliding in a large circle over the grass of the clearing around the person in the center who held the gourd and who turned in the opposite direction. And at the end of each stanza, when

Jasmine began the chorus, the person in the center would toss the gourd to whoever the person was facing and join the others in their large circle. Then they would begin short little hops, clapping their hands and tossing the gourd on to the next person on the left, until the chorus came to an end and the person with the gourd would step into the middle of the clearing. Then they would begin their stately, dignified dance again, celebrating their grace, their power, their freedom. Only Jasmine seemed to be bothered by the wailing from the gourd.

For a long time, the young walker hid in the woods, fascinated by them. But then with all the craft he knew, he circled the clearing quietly—in their walker forms, the owls could not see or hear him—until he came to where they had hung their dresses and robes, flapping like white death shrouds in the trees. Slowly he lifted down the dress that he recognized as one of the sisters', for that one time when his dream-soul had seen the two of them as walkers was burned into his heart. To his surprise he found the dress no heavier than an owl's coat of feathers would be.

Immediately the Owl Spirits stopped dancing.

"Give me the gourd," he told them, "and all but one of you will have back her dress."

"And what if we do not?" asked one of Jasmine's brothers. "What if we attack you instead?"

The young walker showed them his knife. "I will cut as many robes and dresses as I can and some of you will have to walk for the rest of your lives."

Jasmine recognized the dress he held in one hand. "And what will you do with that one?"

"She will become my wife."

Jasmine turned to Peony. "Sister, it must have been destined for him to find us. Or perhaps this happened because we carried our revenge too far. But since it was my idea first to punish him, you may take your dress." Jasmine went to the tree and tossed her own down at his feet.

And so Peony, who held the gourd, crossed the clearing and handed him the gourd, receiving her dress in exchange. Then with a rush, the others ran to the trees, slipping into their dresses and robes, and flew away, humiliated and confused.

The young walker pulled the plug from the gourd and let his brother's souls out. They rose up, like will-o'-the-wisps, shimmering for a moment in the night and then dissipating, free at last. Then the young walker rolled the feather dress up and put it under his arm and Jasmine followed him home to be his wife.

His family never went hungry after that, for Jasmine would walk to the edge of the jungle and call out her sister's name and Peony would flutter down from the shadows, dropping some large munchable like a rabbit for Jasmine to give to her family. And then, too, despite what might have happened before, some of Jasmine's family also pitied her and they would bring her rabbits and small monkeys and other animals to be eaten and fruits as well—though the most expert hunters in the walker clan could find no game nor any fruit or roots in the jungle. And the other families were jealous of the young walker and his Owl-Spirit wife but, for fear of her, they dared do nothing.

And when the gods at last took pity on all creatures, the rains finally swept in from the sea and the rice plants grew again in the fields and the memory of the famine passed as if it had only been a bad dream. And in time the family prospered because of Jasmine's diligent, uncomplaining work, for she worked as hard as the other two brothers. The family bought back their land and house and tools and furniture and even found where the oldest brother was and bought him out of slavery. And for the second brother, they fed his graveside soul and burned the special paper money so that his dream-soul would have plenty of money in the kingdom of the dead.

Perhaps it was because Jasmine had never been an ordinary owl that she was able to adapt to her new life upon the ground. Luckily for her, her husband's mother was not vengeful and showed her the thousand and one things Jasmine must learn now that she walked. And her husband, who would always remain a little shy with her, would do little things for her, such as fetching fresh water for her to use for washing after working in the fields.

Jasmine even came to enjoy life upon the ground, for she was able to express many feelings for her mate that she would have had to keep hidden as an owl. It was a new sensation to be so open about her feelings with someone, and for his part he was equally open with her. Though they mistrusted one another at first, as they worked side by side that mistrust changed to mutual respect and even to admiration and love.

Together they had seven sons, and though it was sometimes exasperating to have so many children about her, more often than not she felt a deep, inner satisfaction in guiding them in their growing instead of having to shove them out of the nest as soon as the children were able to fly and hunt a little, as an owl would have done. Her husband and her children could be a part of her in a way they never would have been had she simply mated and hatched a brood in some jungle nest.

But sometimes when she heard the owls calling to one another, Jasmine would sit down and weep, yearning to be free as she once was. For the blouses and trousers fit her poorly and it was clumsy to have to walk where she had once been able to fly. And sometimes, standing ankle deep in the watery fields, her feet anchored in the black mud, Jasmine would look up at the open sky overhead and be filled with an immense longing to be a part of that openness. And though she watched her husband, he never revealed where he had hidden her dress.

Finally, after some twenty years, she grew tired of walking and got her youngest son, who was the closest to her, to tell a story to her husband about a dress of feathers he must have seen while his dream-soul had been walking. And day after day he mentioned this to his father and this troubled the father.

He questioned the son closely about what the son had seen and heard in the dream. And hidden away, the Owl Spirit listened. And each day she had her son tell of seeing the dress in some new place in the area around their village, until one day she saw her husband start at the mention of the side of the valley.

"Was it the west side or the east side?"

"The west," said his son.

And the husband simply laughed. The day after that, the son said he had seen the dress on the east side and this time the husband did not laugh. "And where did you see it?"

The son, who had been coached by his mother, said, "Perhaps it was by a tree." And when his father started to laugh, the son stopped. "Or perhaps it was a rock."

"Rock, what rock?"

"It was shaped like . . . like . . ." The boy hesitated.

"Like a horse?" the father asked anxiously.

"Yes," said the boy. "Like a horse. Only, while I watched,

a pretty woman came along and lifted up the rock easily and put on the dress and flew away."

Jasmine found the rock before her husband, for she knew the valley well now from having searched it many times before. But she could not lift the heavy rock by herself and so she hid herself in the bushes until her husband came. With difficulty he rolled the rock off a hole in the ground and took out a package wrapped in cloth and inside was the feather dress, fresh and new as the night when he had first stolen it, for the dress was a magical one and the feathers would neither fade nor rot no matter how long they stayed in the ground.

Jasmine had the time to snatch the dress from his hand, but she did not. Instead, she rose from her hiding place and stepped forward. "I am a thousand years old," she said, "and I was never meant to walk on the ground this long. I have worked faithfully by your side and have been respectful to your parents and I have given you sons. Now I would ask you for my dress."

Her husband hesitated, for he truly loved her. "Is it because I've grown older and slower and more wrinkled?" For Jasmine had stayed as beautiful and young as the first day he had captured her.

"It is only that I am tired of walking, always walking," she said. "I really am an owl after all."

And he gave her the dress of his own free will. Eagerly she put on her dress and then looked at him both tenderly and lovingly.

"I thank you for the dress," she said. "It was well given."

And with that she raised her arms over her head and brought them down sharply and in that instant her arms changed to wings and she again took the form of an owl. And her sister Peony slipped out of the shadows and joined her and together they circled once over the man and floated away into the jungle.

When the sad husband returned home, he found his youngest son holding the charm that an owl had just dropped at his feet.

"And all we have is the charm?" I asked Paw-Paw.

"Yes," she said.

Stories don't exactly replace a gas heater; yet some stories can lift you up out of where you are so the cold doesn't seem important anymore. And the story of the owls wasn't even very pleasant—I mean, who wants to go around eating other people and catching souls? But it was like there had always been this person inside of me that I had never been able to name or describe—a small, feathery me lost inside this body—and now I not only knew her name but I could tell part of her story.

Lately, I'd felt guilty when I set out a knife and fork for myself at dinner instead of chopsticks. And at least at first, I was always wishing that I had milk or Coke to drink instead of tea to drink—though eventually I got to like tea. And I knew I talked back to Paw-Paw more than some of the other Chinese kids from my school did to their parents and grandparents. And if I pretended I was an owl, I suddenly had a way of talking about my feelings because I felt like someone who'd been trapped inside the wrong body and among the wrong people.

It was good just to sit next to Paw-Paw, sharing her warmth and knowing I was not alone, that somewhere, at some time, others like me had felt the cold and loneliness. Maybe even like Jeanie, my mom.

Chapter Three

I

I LAY in bed thinking for a long time after Paw-Paw had finished her story. I'd never asked her about Jeanie before this, I suppose, because Barney had taught me not to talk about her. Finally I rolled over on my side to face her. "When did Jeanie feel lonely?"

Paw-Paw picked up a deck of cards and began to play a game of solitaire. She could play even while she talked. A three on the four of one column. A jack on the queen of another column. Flip. Flip. Flip. Like her fingers had eyes and brains so Paw-Paw didn't even have to look down. Her hands could do everything. "Maybe I should let your daddy tell you."

I turned so I lay on my stomach, hugging a pillow under my chin. "Barney won't talk much about her. Was she lonely when she was my age?"

Paw-Paw must have sensed the longing in my voice. "Oh, no. Your mommy always had lots of friends. She was very pretty. And very sweet. She was always a big help to me." Paw-Paw finished her game and began to sweep the cards into the middle of the table so she could gather them into a deck. "And your daddy was thought to be a very good-looking boy so they were always a natural couple. From grammar school on."

"Grammar school?"

"They both went to Commodore Stockton just a little way from here. And then they went through junior high and high school together." Paw-Paw began to shuffle her cards to get them ready for the next time she wanted to play.

"Were they very popular?"

"Oh, yes. Very popular. You'd always see them together at all the dances in Chinatown. Your momma liked dancing."

Paw-Paw went to the bureau and opened a middle drawer, rummaging around till she took out an old, worn brown bag and drew a small pile of photos out of it. She set them down on the table and sorted through them. "That's your momma. She was going to a dance that night." Paw-Paw tapped one photo of a pretty girl of about sixteen in bobby sox and a long skirt like all the American girls used to wear—or at least that's what Barney and some of the older people used to tell me when we had watched late-night movies in different hotel lobbies. "I used to sew all your momma's clothes but only with the best material."

She glanced at me briefly and then went through some of the other old photos of Jeanie, who had a different outfit in each one. And while I didn't much care about the clothes, somehow talking with Paw-Paw about Jeanie made me feel less lonely.

"But she couldn't have always gone out with Barney. What did she do with you for fun? I mean, besides playing cards."

"We went to see Chinese movies." Paw-Paw put her cards down in a neat stack by the little cup that held her toothpicks. They were cinnamon-flavored and each was wrapped in a little paper envelope. "Would you like to see a movie like your mommy and I used to see?"

I wasn't doing much of anything so I figured why not. "I've got money for myself."

"Why spend your money? I can sew some extra shirts this week."

"Are you sure it's okay?" I asked.

"Of course, it's okay," she snapped and I could see there would be no arguing with her.

Paw-Paw bundled up as usual, putting on a blouse over her pajama top and then a sweater and a heavy silk jacket over the sweater so that by the time she had on her heavy cloth coat, she looked twice as round. Over her head she put her favorite vermillion chiffon scarf with the roses embroidered on it with gold thread.

Paw-Paw seemed very comfortable within the small world of Chinatown; I wondered if Jeanie had been too. It didn't cover more than half a square mile or so then, and within those boundaries, as I was to find out, it is a very small, tightly knit world where everyone knows your business and you know theirs. To the west lay the souvenir shops and on the east, delicatessens and grocery stores and meat markets, some of which had fish tanks in the bottom half of their windows in which a hundred fish would be squeezed, all staring out at you with cold, black eyes, or even turtles, or sometimes cages of snakes, all to be sold and eaten.

To the north was Stockton Street, where my school was. Mostly it was sewing-machine shops up that way: plain storefronts sometimes with wallpaper covering the windows or old, sun-bleached curtains. From within would come the steady whir and whine of the machines of the ladies sewing dresses, shirts, even jeans and expensive wedding outfits for American stores. A lot of ladies with no English could only do that. Just above Stockton Street was the public grammar school, Commodore Stockton, or "Commodore" to the kids. Across from it lay the YWCA and Cameron House, a kind of club for Chinese kids. Above that, where Paw-Paw never went, were the cable-car lines and the apartment houses for Americans, including the fancy hotels and limousines of Nob Hill.

To the south lay Paw-Paw's club, as she called it, but I'll tell you about that later.

But at that moment I was thinking mainly about the movies we were going to see. I had my doubts because all I had seen up to then were Charlie Chan movies or silly houseboys on TV shows or funny laundrymen in westerns. But even so, one of those kinds of movies was better than nothing because I knew Paw-Paw never left Chinatown to see any of the Hollywood movies just a few blocks away.

We went to the Chinese Globe that had a bright neon sign outside in front and looked like a regular theater except for the fact that there was a guy selling newspapers by the ticket booth. He had about a dozen different Chinese newspapers laid in neat piles on a board that he laid over some boxes. But I saw a dozen portable newsstands like that set up all over Chinatown—in doorways or in corners or in front of busy stores. He nodded familiarly to Paw-Paw as she bought our tickets at the booth.

When I finally got to see the movies, they were completely different than I thought. I could see why Jeanie had liked them. For one thing, the Chinese were actually people who could be brave or sad. They had subtitles in English, too, which was good. It was something to see Chinese do more than be the sidekick to some white guy in a fight, or see the Chinese actually win. I mean, I almost felt like crying when I saw it: a kind of bubbling feeling deep down inside that had me almost cheering and crying while this Chinese mother led her three sons in beating up the bad guys. And it was even better when I saw the Chinese girls fighting.

The second feature, you see, was *Princess of the Streets*, which is about this girl who grows up in the back streets of Hong Kong and all the pimps and whores and toughs she knows. She gets friendly with this other girl who does juggling and fighting displays in a medicine show. And together she and her friend wipe out the big crime boss. I don't think I ever saw anyone jump as high in the air to kick someone.

It must have rained while we were inside the theater because when we came out later, the streets were slick and black, like they were made of shining crystal. I saw a Chinatown I'd never seen before. It was the Chinatown Jeanie must have seen. Suddenly all the gaudy neon signs were no longer a bunch of words but were like snakes of colored lights crawling up the faces of the buildings and their reflections smashed themselves on the streets, looking like broken stars sliding back and forth and trying to put themselves back together. Funny, but it seemed, right then, like I'd just come home.

A radio store had begun playing music over an outside loudspeaker. Some of the stuff, especially the opera, sounded terrible to me—a high whiney kind of noise—but this sounded different. Some people might have thought there was too much of a clutter of sound with the cymbals crashing and the drums beating and everybody playing like mad, but there was something inside of me that liked it—like it synchronized right with the pulsing of my blood through my body. And the sound wound its way through the chatter of the nighttime crowds.

Humming with the tune, Paw-Paw took my arm for support as we made our way along the slippery pavements of Grant Avenue. We passed by the delicatessens, where Paw-Paw pointed to the dark-brown, roasted ducks dangling from hooks in the windows. "That's what I like," she said. "Jeanie too."

"I've never had duck in my life," I said.

She patted my arm, the one she was holding on to. "Maybe I'll sew some extra shirts and dresses someday and we'll buy half of one so you can try it."

We went about two blocks before the rain started to fall again. It was falling pretty hard so we stopped under the awning of this one souvenir shop. Paw-Paw acted like the window display had been put there just to entertain us. "Look at that whirly thing." She pointed at one of those little solar windmills that rotate whenever they're near a source of light like the light bulb illuminating the window.

There was something wrong about the window. At first I couldn't figure it out but as Paw-Paw went on mentioning things in the window, I realized she hadn't talked about one Chinese thing yet. I started to study the window then. There didn't seem to be anything as beautiful or as old as the owl charm Paw-Paw wore about her neck. There was just a lot of silly stuff like two-headed back scratchers, or gross things like playing cards with nude women, or salt shakers that were the left and right breasts of a nude statue, or battery-powered dogs urinating and so on. Paw-Paw didn't point at any of those or at some of the things that were downright nasty—like pellet guns and various types of knives, from simple pocket- and hunting knives to switchblades and gravity blades that snap out with a flick of a wrist. The only thing vaguely Oriental that I saw at first in the window were the Japanese kimonos and geisha dolls they sold.

"It doesn't seem right somehow," I said. "I mean, if it's a Chinatown souvenir shop, shouldn't it be selling Chinese stuff?"

"The Americans won't let us bring in things from China." She shrugged. "And the Taiwan government's too busy to bother with souvenirs. You have to sell the Americans something."

"But we're selling things as if they're Chinese when it's really . . . well, I don't know . . . this stuff just seems like junk compared to your owl charm. There's no story behind most of this stuff. There's no meaning to this stuff. This junk is probably not even much fun."

"They do have a few real Chinese things. See?" She moved a little to the side and bent down, pointing to one dark corner of the window. "See down there in the back?"

I leaned forward slightly and looked where her finger was pointing and saw a bunch of dusty statues crowded together like they were making a last stand. "They've got some of the stuff you've got on your bureau. Look, there's that pretty lady with the flower."

Paw-Paw studied me. I hadn't laughed about the owl story and I had even liked the Chinese movies so I guess she decided to go ahead. "That lady is the Listener. She could have gone to heaven, but when she was just about to enter the gate, she could hear all the poor souls back on earth groaning and she turned her back on heaven, saying she could not enter until everyone else had gone before her, so she spends all her time trying to help the rest of us to heaven."

Though it was a cold, rainy night outside, I felt warm inside now that Paw-Paw was finally explaining things to me. "Hey, there's the guy with the big head."

"He's the spirit of long life," Paw-Paw corrected me. "His head swelled up because he's so full of life. He helps keep the record of your life and sometimes with special people he juggles his books and they live longer, so maybe someone dies when they're ninety-one instead of nineteen. He's got a magic peach in his hand, grown in heaven for the gods. A person eats that peach and that person lives forever."

And she told me the eight statues—not as small as hers— were the Eight Immortals who had once been simple men and women but had gained the secret of immortality. One of them had meditated so long and let his dream-soul wander so far away that his body died in the meantime and his dream-soul had to take the bony body of a crippled beggar when it got back.

She told me about a few more of the statues and when she stopped, I asked her a new question I'd been thinking about. "What would it be like if we were in China, Paw-Paw?"

Paw-Paw shut her eyes but kept her face turned toward the window as if she were trying to picture it herself. "It'd be very noisy and you'd have much less time to yourself than here. You have to go through the rain to the village lavatory. Or maybe you have to empty out a . . . a . . . what is the word? . . . a chamber pot."

"Ugh."

"No heat except the stuff in the stove so you have to go and look for every leaf and every bit of grass and all your neighbors would be doing the same thing."

"Would you have a whole bunch of families together in the same big house? Like Uncle Phil and Uncle Chester would live with you?" Uncle Chester was a year younger than Jeanie and lived down in L.A.

Paw-Paw shook her head. "Only if we were rich, but we'd probably be poor farmers if we had stayed back in China. Each of them would have their own little house and you and I would be crowded in somehow into one of those two."

I drew my finger down the glass slowly. Rain dribbled down from the awning overhead. "But still, would you like that better than the way you live now? I mean if we were in China, you'd really be in charge, like the mother was in the first movie, bossing all her grown-up sons around."

Paw-Paw sighed. "I don't know. It's too easy to worry about the way things might have been. I'd rather live with the way things are now. That's what the Owl Spirit did after all."

"Well, why don't you live with one of your children now?"

"I could live with your Uncle Phil anytime I want, but they always get this rotten chicken meat from the freezer, when chickens should be fresh. But no, the feathers make too much mess and they don't like it when I take out the blood and guts. And I say, 'What do you think's inside of you?' Or they give me steak in a huge chunk and they hand me a knife and that thing with the four sharp points."

"A fork?"

"Yes, and I say, 'When I come to the dinner table, I come to eat, not to cook. Meat should be cut up and cooked properly in the kitchen before dinner.'"

"They'd probably let you make your own meals," I said.

"Well, I guess I could make my peace with them on that, but there are other things." Her eyes glanced at the statues in the window. "They tell me those things are only for stupid, old people."

I realized that it all depended on how I looked around myself—if there were invisible walls around Chinatown for Paw-Paw, they were like the walls of a turtle, walls behind which you could remain warm and alive, and for someone like me, those walls didn't have to be any more of a trap than I let them. They could be like something to give me shape and form and when I couldn't grow anymore inside them, I could break out of those invisible walls.

Paw-Paw began to retie her scarf but her fingers had begun to stiffen in the cold and the wet. I reached my hands out. "Here, Paw-Paw, let me help you." So Paw-Paw leaned forward, waiting patiently until I had retied her scarf. She checked the knot under the chin of her reflection in the window, smoothing her hand over it.

She smiled, pleased. "You did that very well. Such strong young fingers."

She gripped my fingers tightly in her hand for a moment with what seemed like an immense strength. "Now help an old lady up the hill. It's wet and I'm afraid I'm going to fall."

I let her take my arm then and once again she was just a little old lady and we climbed slowly up the steeply slanting hillside, like two small owls clawing their way along a branch that twisted upward into the night sky.

II

WE slept late the next day until the bells from Old St. Mary's began ringing. "Paw-Paw, are you awake?"

She half opened one eye, murmuring drowsily. "No."

"Come on, Paw-Paw. You know you never really answered my question yesterday."

"You asked many questions. Which one?"

"You know. When did Jeanie really start feeling lonely? Was it . . . when Barney started gambling?"

"Yes, that was many years after they left school and got married."

"High school?"

"Yes. When he started gambling, he started to leave her alone.

She talked to him about it and he got mad and left her alone even more often."

"Geezus, that was stupid. Why did Barney start gambling?"

Paw-Paw turned onto her back, pulling the covers up about both our necks. "I'm not sure. It would be better if I introduce you to a friend of mine. He used to see a lot of your daddy because your daddy and his nephew were best friends and used to hang around the store where my friend used to work. So your daddy might have talked to my friend about that gambling stuff more than your daddy did to me or Jeanie. My friend works in a restaurant now washing dishes but today he has his rest."

We had a leisurely brunch in a little restaurant, ordering one plate of chow mein that fed us both, and then, after we had bought some vegetables and put them in our shopping bag, we went down to Paw-Paw's club. A lot of older Chinese belonged to such social clubs; some of them even rented buildings along Waverly Place. Some were for men only, though some were mixed. And in the evenings, I'd hear the sound of people practicing their musical instruments, or go past some cellar door with the iron doors thrown back to let out the smoke and heat and I'd hear the clacking of Mah-Jong tiles and the loud voices of the players.

Paw-Paw never went further south than Kearny and Portsmouth Square. They've remodeled the square since then, adding a lot of playground equipment and benches and tables; but at that time it was just a half block of grassy lawn fronting the Hall of Justice. Paw-Paw's group was too poor to afford the high rents for their very own building so they met down at the square.

If the sun is going to shine anyplace in San Francisco, it will shine in Chinatown. Paw-Paw says it's because the early Chinese, when they first settled on the sand dunes, chose the sunny east side of the hills because it felt right. But to be honest with you, I think it's because we've got a bunch of hills between us and the ocean fog. It's foggy most of the time on the other side of the peninsula but the clouds don't always get past the hills or if they do, they burn away. And if the sun shines anywhere in Chinatown, it will be in Portsmouth Square, so that the square was more than a plain little green square surrounded on all sides by tall buildings. It seemed more like the green bottom of a large empty pool in which the light welled up.

Generally, the women took one part of the square, the men the other part. The more old-fashioned would never think of mixing with the opposite sex the way the members of Paw-Paw's club did.

Even in Paw-Paw's club, the women and men sat more or less separately. The women sat gossiping loudly about their friends still living or dead while the men sat on benches, a piece of paper spread out before them with grids on it and a blue line through the middle. Paw-Paw told me they were playing Chinese chess. Instead of chessmen, they moved little discs, each of which had a character on it—like a chariot or general and so on. Men stood around the players kibitzing or grunting "*Hou*" when someone made a good move.

Besides the groups of men and women, you would see solitary figures standing by themselves. Old men in worn, patched gray work clothes rooted through the garbage cans, looking for something they could use. I was sure they crinkled when they moved—I suppose they wore rolled-up newspapers around their bodies to help them keep warm. Barney had told me about that old hobo's trick once.

And one old woman sat by herself on a bench shouting out to no one in particular. Paw-Paw told me she was crazy. But all of them would at some time sit and stare emptily at the traffic passing by on the street below as if they were lost inside their own memories, trying to understand how they found themselves old and alone, sitting on a bench—with the look of people who had been left behind on some grassy shore when the ship had sailed. Only it was more than an ocean they had to cross, it was time and space itself.

Paw-Paw walked directly toward one set of benches where a group of women sat talking. They called out greetings to one another and then Paw-Paw introduced me to them in Chinese. They all beamed at me, nodding their heads. It seemed to add to both my and Paw-Paw's stature for me to come down with her.

Feeling out of place like an owl, I stood around without the slightest idea of what Paw-Paw was talking about, when one little woman said something shyly to me. She snapped open her purse and took out a small, rectangular black-and-white photograph of several Chinese children. From the date on the side of the photograph, I could see it had been developed ten years ago. "These my grandchildren," she said proudly. "They come see me today. Soon." She was to show me the photo and repeat the story several times when I was there. It was only later that Paw-Paw told me she always said that every day. Nobody ever came.

"Where's the man?" I whispered to Paw-Paw.

"There. But we mustn't disturb him."

I saw an elderly man in an old, three-piece, navy-blue suit get up from a bench. Any tears in his suit had been painstakingly repaired and it looked clean—probably because he brushed it with a wet cloth and ironed it every night. The old man began to move with impressive dignity, his legs and arms bending and shifting, flowing into one figure of an exercise and then into the next, as fierce and proud and graceful as a hawk.

I sat down by Paw-Paw. "What's he doing?"

"Shhh, girl. That's Mr. Jeh. He's doing *Tai Chi*, the Grand Ultimate Exercises."

"It looks like he's dancing."

"He's . . ." Paw-Paw struggled for the words. "He's flowing. You know. You breathe in and move with the energy of the world so it can energize you. See how he always moves first with his waist. That's where all the strength comes from."

And then Paw-Paw told me some of his story. He had once been a man of property back at home but had lost everything, including his wife and children, in the Communist Revolution of 1949. His brother had brought his family over here and his nephews in turn had their own families, but he refused to live with any of them. Instead he earned his keep by washing dishes and by what he got from social security. He stayed in an old ramshackle hotel just down Kearny, sharing a room with two other men. They had a kitchen they shared with the rest of the floor—though Mr. Jeh usually ate his meals at the restaurant where he worked. Today, though, was his day off.

He finished all the figures just before noon and for a time he stood very still as if he had to bring himself back into this world slowly. Then he looked up and you could see the bright, lively look in his eyes as he walked toward us in the typical posture of an old Chinese, his hands clasped behind his back, his head bent forward slightly, and shuffling. It wasn't the most manly posture in the world, and yet he seemed somehow unbreakable. Compared to him, John Wayne was a blown-up balloon about to explode.

"Mr. Jeh, this is my granddaughter," Paw-Paw said.

He nodded his head. "Pleased to meet you," he said.

"She saw her first *kung fu* movie the other day." Paw-Paw pronounced the word *kung* in a different way than I'd seen it spelled—more like *goong*.

"You never see one before?" He seemed amused. "Where you been, Child of Owl? They keep you in closet?"

I suppose he knew about the charm that belonged to our family and somehow it made me feel warm inside. "Do you know *kung fu*?" I asked excitedly.

"A little, but I no . . . no martial artist like in movies. This is *Tai Chi*. I do it more for *spirit* of thing." He said *spirit* as if satisfied he'd found the right word. But that didn't really help me any.

"What does it feel like then?"

"Like . . . like the ground holding you up. Most people, it not matter to them where they are. They could be over nothing and if they not fall, they not notice, not care. But the ground can hold you up. Hold up." He repeated himself to make sure I got the point. I didn't—not then. But I asked him some more questions to be polite and he answered all of them, seeming pleased that a young person would be curious, and when I thanked him for his patience, he smiled and shook his head. "It make me happy talk to you." And he added something in Chinese.

I looked at him blankly.

He glanced at Paw-Paw, realizing for the first time that I didn't know Chinese, and Paw-Paw shifted on the bench uncomfortably. "I tell you," Mr. Jeh said carefully, "that most native-born no brains." He added, "Even my own nephews and nieces and grandnephews and grandnieces, they laugh at me. All this stuff, they say, it only for stubborn old fools." Mr. Jeh paused dramatically. "You know, they not even believe I lose one of my souls."

I blinked. "Pardon?"

"She doesn't know those kind of things," Paw-Paw said quickly.

"Then maybe she should learn so she know what to watch out for," Mr. Jeh chided Paw-Paw. He turned to me. "You see, everyone born with two souls. When you sleep, one soul, it leave the body and wander in other places, other times. That's what dreams are. And sometimes you get sick, same thing happen. But sometimes maybe some bad ghost, he get into your body and shut out the soul that wandering. The soul that left behind, it too dumb or too weak or too scared to do anything."

"Remember that one immortal who had to become a crippled beggar?" Paw-Paw explained.

Mr. Jeh coughed, hawked, and spat neatly into the bushes. Then he dabbed politely at his mouth with a Kleenex, which he pitched into a trash can next to the bench. "Once, ten years ago, I very, very sick. I not remember any of this. The others, they tell me about this. Some ghost take over my body when I sick.

At first my friends, they think I get better, but I not remember their names. And . . ." He paused melodramatically. "I am so surprised to be living where I am, or eating the foods I ate."

Paw-Paw laughed. "He had the ghost of a rich man in him, you see."

"At first, the ghost, he try to find some better place to live, but no can—not on my money. Then he try live with my nephews and nieces but that even worse. Eventually, the ghost, he got so tired of it, he leave my body. So my own soul get back in and join my other one again."

Silently pleading, Paw-Paw looked at me. He sounded a little crazy to me, but not in any bad way. And if I accepted certain of his assumptions, it even kind of made sense. He seemed like a kind enough man and I didn't see what harm he could do.

"That's really too bad," I said. Paw-Paw looked relieved. "Mr. Jeh's nephew and Barney were very good friends," she explained again to me.

Mr. Jeh nodded his head. "You bet."

"Can you tell me why Barney started to gamble?" I asked.

Mr. Jeh eyed Paw-Paw, who nodded her head ever so slightly. "Don't blame your daddy. His luck, it was always bad." Mr. Jeh sighed. "Very bad. Each of us has only a certain amount of luck we're born with. Some have a lot. Others don't have any. He used up all of his going to school. He got all good marks. All A's. But when he get out, only job maybe as houseboy."

He stopped, his face taking on a fierce expression as we heard a loud roaring sound like a dragon falling out of the skies. This bright-purple Cadillac with huge fins on the back tore up Kearny Street right past the police like the driver was the president himself. He took the corner on two wheels, the chassis slamming back down as he turned up the street. He halted by a red zone and, in a smooth curve backward, parked smooth and easy right next to the painted curb. Beside him was a plump Chinese girl with two pounds of makeup on her eyes and a bee-hive hairdo that added maybe a foot to her height.

When the driver got out, I saw he was a young man in his twenties. "I told you, I want to hear the Airplane. They knock me out."

"But I don't want to go to the Matrix." The girl, wearing a tight, short skirt and a frilly blouse, slid across the seat and got out. "Everyone looks and acts funny in that nightclub. And what kind of band calls itself the Jefferson Airplane?"

"Pick you up at eight," the driver said. The girl looked like she wanted to argue some more but the young man ignored her. She walked away in a huff, her heels clicking on the sidewalk. There was something familiar about him when he strolled over to us. He moved in a slouching swagger like Errol Flynn trying to walk after getting kicked in the gut. He was wearing a pink shirt and skintight black jeans and a black Windbreaker. His heavily pomaded hair swept back and up and was arranged into winglike sides. He seemed like a cross between some pachukes I knew up in Stockton and a Chinese kid: a Pachinko.

Mr. Jeh turned his back and pretended to be absorbed in the chess game on the bench a few feet away.

"Hey, old man," the Pachinko mumbled.

Mr. Jeh shifted uncomfortably on the bench but said nothing.

"How are you today, Gilbert?" Paw-Paw asked politely.

The Pachinko slouched against a lamppost and managed to hook a thumb into the top of his pants—I didn't see how, seeing how tight they already were. "Fine, fine, Mrs. Low, and yourself?" he mumbled.

"Pretty good for an old woman."

He stroked his jaw with the thumb of his free hand and went on mumbling. "Old? Bet you could dance the shoes off me. Hey, what about me and you going to the next dance up at the Chinese Center?"

"That's past my bedtime."

The Pachinko laughed vaguely and nodded. He took out a cigarette and let it dangle from his lips like it was just about to fall out. I couldn't place him until he started the bit with the cigarette, but finally I recognized him as a poor-man's brand of James Dean, that punk kid who made all those *Rebel Without a Cause* movies. He jerked his head at me.

"You want something, kid?"

"This is my granddaughter."

"No kidding." He stuck out a hand and I shook it. "In that sweat shirt and jeans, you could have fooled me."

"Say, just how many pounds of lard do you use a week?" I asked.

"Casey!" Paw-Paw said sternly.

"I started it," the Pachinko grinned lopsidedly. "Let's start again, okay?"

" 'Kay."

"My name's Gilbert. What's yours, kid?"

"Casey Young," I said.

"Casey it is." He grinned slightly—like he wanted to take it easy on his face muscles.

"There's a cop coming." I saw one of the white-helmeted motorcycle cops come chugging up the hill on a three-wheeler. Gilbert checked out the cop and then turned back to us, shrugging lazily. "It's okay." With an elaborately casual air, he took out a matchbook and using just the fingers of one hand, bent a match outwards, sliding the flap back between the match and the others. Then he lit the match one-handed by resting the matchbook in the palm of his hand while his thumb struck the match against the black strip. Holding the match and matchbook up to his mouth, he lit his cigarette. He talked a little bit more with Paw-Paw while the cop chugged on by up the hill. It was like the purple Cadillac was never there—a little hard to believe but there you are.

Finally the Pachinko took out a wad of bills about as big as my fist. He peeled off five tens and dropped them on the ground. "Bye now, Mrs. Low. Kid." He winked at me and then swaggered on back to his purple Caddie. Paw-Paw waited until he slammed the door shut and had twisted his car away from the curb before she bent over and picked up the money. She folded the money neatly and picked up Mr. Jeh's coat, which he must have laid down on the bench when he had been exercising. Everyone in the club had either gone on playing chess or talking with one another, politely not noticing. It didn't take a genius to know I wasn't supposed to notice either.

Mr. Jeh suddenly looked up from the chess game right at me and then turned to Paw-Paw. "You're lucky to have a good girl like her for a grandchild."

"Some of your family show respect."

Mr. Jeh snorted. "Like that Gilbert? Who can keep track of his doings? Sheridan, his father, should do that but he too busy; he want add more empty whiskey bottles to his collection. Work all day in Orange Julius, spend all night drinking up what he earn."

"Whenever something goes wrong in Chinatown, you think it's Gilbert or his father," Paw-Paw scolded him.

Mr. Jeh replied in Chinese and they held the rest of the conversation that way so I didn't understand it.

But the moment we were out of earshot and heading for home, I asked if the Pachinko was really Mr. Jeh's grandnephew.

"Yes. In fact, Gilbert is the son of Barney's friend." Paw-Paw added, "Gilbert drives that big car for a professional gambler. They play games with dice and the game switches from one place to another, so that the players have to be picked up by him and taken there. He gets a lot of tips from the gamblers who win because it's important to share your good luck when you win. Every month Gilbert leaves money but Mr. Jeh won't take his money. He leaves it in his coat and the unlucky members of the club take what they need from his coat pocket."

"Unlucky?"

"Men and women who have lost their families or whose families have lost them."

"Lost them?"

"Thrown them aside. That seems to happen more and more nowadays."

"Have you ever taken his money, Paw-Paw?"

"I've been doing all right." Paw-Paw stopped for a moment to knock on the wooden frame of a store window. It was funny how the American things Paw-Paw found easiest to learn were superstitions.

"But Mr. Jeh should thank Gilbert at least."

"Gilbert is a good young man but a bit careless."

"Do you think Gilbert has some owl as an ancestor?"

Paw-Paw smiled patiently. "If you think about the Chinese over here that way, I guess we all have. But we don't have to have owls as ancestors. We became a little like owls the moment we turned our backs on China and the old ways."

The shopping bag in my hand brushed against my leg rhythmically as we walked up the hill.

III

THAT next weekend I went into the Orange Julius on Grant. There were two clerks; one was a kid of about twenty; the other was a man in his forties that I figured must be Sheridan. There was also the ponytailed girl from school sitting at the counter. At first I wasn't going to go in and then suddenly I realized that I had as much right to be here as she did. After all, wasn't I a child of the owl? I even sat down on the stool next to her.

I knew more about her now from Paw-Paw. Booger wasn't her real name. Her rich great-aunt, who couldn't speak much English, had named her Tallulah Bankhead after her favorite

actress. Her aunt happened to be the lady who owned the building we lived in and she let Booger and her family stay there provided they collected the rent and kept the place up.

Booger would have gone through life known as Tallulah except for the fact that back in the first grade she had once taken
a hairpin out of her hair to pick her nose. The kids had all
started calling her Booger after that and the name had stuck
until almost everyone, including her brothers and sisters, called
her Booger.

On her lap she had a majorette's baton. The school had a
girls' drum corps where all the girls dressed up in silk outfits
with sequins and marched in parades. I suppose she'd been at
one of their Saturday-morning practices.

"What do you want?" The man came over, his face wearing a
sullen, slightly hung-over expression—I suppose the loud rock
music the kid was playing on his radio didn't help any.

And suddenly I felt this craving for a hamburger. After meals
of vegetables and rice and a few strips of meat, I wanted a soft,
brown bun spongy white on the inside with preservatives and a
crisp, hard hamburger and a bunch of stringy french fries that I
could eat one by one after I had dipped each one in salt and
ketchup. I still had a few bucks from the money Morey had
loaned me. "A hamburger and fries, please."

He grunted and shuffled over toward the grill, throwing a
killing glance at the kid sitting and humming on the stool. So
far the kid had only sat on his stool behind the counter and
read the green sports page from the *Chronicle* and maybe nodded his head now and then—slightly out of time—to the music
on his portable radio.

I turned then to Booger. We weren't in school now and there
weren't any nuns around to protect her. We were actually the
same height, but I felt big and owlish while she seemed small
and mous-ish. "You say one word about the way I'm dressed
and I'll wrap that baton around your neck."

She sipped so hard on her drink that the cords stood out on
her throat. She did her best to look straight ahead. I put my
elbow on the table and leaned forward so I could rest my head
against my hand and study her. "*D-d-dr—ggggg.*" She made the
funny noise drawing the last sip from her drink. She risked a
glance to the side and saw I was still there. I guess she was
scared to move past me. She pushed her glass toward the man.
"Another please." Sullenly he took it and filled it with another
Orange Julius, which is like a glass of orange juice jazzed up

with something like melted vanilla ice cream.

He brought it back along with my order.

"Can I have a small Julius too?" I asked.

"Why'n't you say so before?" he complained. He went and made another, slapping the glass down along with the check. "You can pay now."

"You Sheridan?"

"What of it?" He jerked his head at me.

I gave him the money. "Did you know a Barney Young when you were a kid?"

"Maybe," Sheridan said carefully. After he gave me back the change, he picked up a towel and began wiping the counter top even though it was already clean.

"I'm his kid," I said.

He took off his little paper cap and wiped at the sweat on his forehead with the back of his hand. Then he planted the paper cap carefully back on his head. There were five little, greasy ovals now from his fingers. I guess I knew where his son got the grease for his hair. "I don't have any money to loan him," he warned me.

"He doesn't need your money," I said quickly. "Everything's going right for him. Just like in the old days when you and he were in school."

"Yeah? I'm glad to hear that." Sheridan's face softened a bit. "Those were the best years of our lives when we were in high school." He shook his head regretfully, looking at some spot over my head. "It was a shock when we got out. Right in the middle of the Depression."

"Yeah? Got knocked around a lot?"

Sheridan went back to his aimless wiping of the counter. "You know it. But I think it was always harder on him. Me, I wasn't smart like him so I never expected nothing but shit jobs. But him, he and Jeanie always aced everything and then they got married right away. Real cute. Went around to all the same offices and it was always the same story. The boss'd offer her a job but not him."

"But why?"

"Most American bosses are men who'll hire a pretty Chinese girl just like that." Sheridan snapped his fingers. "But to hell with some uppity Chinese boy. Let him stay a houseboy." He threw down the towel suddenly and went to the black, burnt metal sheet of the grill. He scraped at it nervously with the spatula. "He took it for maybe ten years, but it was eating away at him inside. And then, oh, I guess about the time the war ended, he said, to hell with it. See, it was like there was this brick wall in front of us. Some guys like me knew we couldn't get past it so we never tried. And you got your other guys who just went on beating their heads against it for years and years, but it was like Barney gave up because he'd paid his dues and now somebody owed him something."

"Who?"

"I don't know." Sheridan set the spatula aside and leaned forward on his folded arms across the counter. "Maybe God. Maybe whatever runs the world. But it was like Barney figured all he had to do was be patient now and everything would come to him."

"That's when he started . . ." I glanced at Booger. "Well, you know, doing that stuff." Sheridan understood that I meant gambling.

"Yeah," he said.

Poor Barney.

The kid lowered his paper. "Hey, I told you to get the straws from the back."

"Yeah. Yeah," Sheridan said. He started to turn back to talk to me.

"I mean *now*," the kid said. He turned his radio down. "Look. I haven't told my dad about your coming in late in the mornings so hung over you can barely tell the spatula from the hamburger. But I'm not going to let you loaf around all day."

For a moment I could see the helpless, angry frustration in Sheridan's face, and then that same sullen, pained expression I had seen before snapped back into place like a mask. He heaved himself up from the counter wearily. "Yeah. Yeah. See ya around, kid." He walked with maddening slowness into the storeroom behind the counter in the back. The kid turned up the radio and started to read his paper again.

I started to eat my hamburger slowly, savoring every crunchy, greasy, unnutritious bite.

"I wish you'd go away," Booger said, looking straight ahead. "You're making me so nervous I'm breaking my diet."

"Nobody's stopping you."

She began to sip at her Orange Julius. Looking up at the menu overhead, she said, "I bet you couldn't wrap the baton around my neck. I mean, just because you wear a sweat shirt and jeans doesn't mean you're tough."

"When you lug around a bag of newspapers or when you help

stock shelves in stores, you don't worry much about how you dress."

She began to pick at the napkins in the holder, her fingers beginning to shred the corners of the front one while it was still in the holder. "You've done that?"

"We had to eat."

She frowned as if that was kind of hard to understand. "What does your dad do?"

I didn't think Booger could have made much out of my conversation with Sheridan. "Stuff." I shrugged. "But it never pays well. He keeps trying to make these deals, see. So we gotta keep moving around. Fresno. Los Angeles. Stockton."

"Jeez, you've been around. I'd have never left San Francisco except for that old drum corps. And, then, all I see is a lot of people on the street watching the parade."

"You like being in it?"

"Yeah, but I think I'll quit. All these morning practices are getting to be murder."

I took a sip of my Orange Julius, which was cool and frosty. It was good to get my mind off Barney and Jeanie for a while. "Then why don't you quit?"

"I need something that'll make me exercise."

"Play basketball or volleyball."

She shoved her glasses back up her nose. "I'm always afraid of breaking my glasses and getting the glass fragments in my eyes." She made a face.

"You read that in *Vault of Horror*?" I asked, suddenly interested.

"Had to read my cousin's comic. My mom won't let me buy them. Says they're not *wholesome*." She made a face on the last word. "All she'll let me read about is a lot of fuzzy little animals."

"Running around without any pants on and bashing each other over the head."

Booger stared straight in front of her for a moment and then she began to grin as if she couldn't help herself. Even though she put her hand over her mouth, I could hear her giggling; and the sound of her giggling got me to think about Donald Duck in pants and Tweety Bird in diapers. I started to giggle too until both of us were rolling over the counter.

Booger turned the glass slowly around in a circle between her palms. "This is terrible. I'll never be able to read one of those comics again without getting the giggles."

"You're supposed to giggle at them. They're funny, fuzzy little animals. Remember? And if you still get dirty thoughts, you just tell me and I'll paint jeans over Bugs Bunny for you."

That touched off a fresh round of giggles till the kid frowned and sighed, turning up the rock music on his transistor radio even louder than before. I remembered how hungry I was and so I finished my hamburger.

Booger dawdled over her Orange Julius, sipping more quietly this time at the dregs in her glass. "You doing anything afterwards?"

"Going to do my homework."

"Sure you are."

"Aren't you?" I tried to ask with a straight face but I could feel the beginnings of another laugh slip through the corners of my mouth.

"Want to come and check out a dirty-book store with me then?"

"Does it have lots of comics with half-naked animals?"

"Plenty. Also the latest issue of *Wonder Woman*." Wonder Woman was the Amazon princess who used her superstrength and magic weapons to fight bad guys and monsters from all over the universe.

I twirled around the rest of my Orange Julius. "Has she found that shmuck Steve yet?" Steve Trevor was Wonder Woman's boyfriend.

"No, I think the Martians still have him prisoner."

"I don't know what she sees in that drip anyway. He always makes things twice as hard for her."

"She loves him," Booger said as if that explained all. She slipped the straw out, tapping it on the side so not a drop would be wasted. Then she drained the very last bit of her Orange Julius from the glass.

When I got down to the bottom of my glass, the straw made a loud, ratchety sound as I drew on it. The kid frowned and turned the radio up louder. I pretended to take a deep breath to really drag on the straw and he turned the sound up to an ear-splitting volume. But instead of making a loud noise—which I doubt he would have heard now—I only sipped very genteelly on the straw and set the glass down on the counter. For the sake of his hangover, I hoped Sheridan couldn't hear much in the storeroom.

Booger was waiting in the doorway. "Why did you do that?" she asked as we stepped outside. "You can hear 'A Hard Day's Night' up and down Grant."

"Advertising," I said. "I want the Beatles to enter the minds and hearts of all America. It's part of my plan."

"Plan for what?"

"Instead of the national anthem, we'll have to sing 'A Hard Day's Night' and everybody but everybody is going to have to wear roller skates or wind up headfirst in Elvis Presley's own personal vat of Vaseline."

"Ugh," Booger said, but she began to giggle. I started to like her because it was awful easy to get her to laugh. We went over to her local pusher of trash for the young minds of America, a little old lady who couldn't count money too good and depended on the kids to help her add up the cost of the comics. Not many people tried to cheat her because she was good about letting you read comics all day without buying anything. And when a kid tried to cheat, usually another kid pointed out the "mistake."

It was a jumbled-up little shop with stairs that led upstairs to where the lady slept. There were comics covering one small wall of the shop and gossip magazines on the other with several boxes of bubble-gum cards in front and lots of candy. There were little toys too and little trinkets like spaceman key rings.

The *Wonder Woman* wasn't in yet, but the latest *Katy Keene* was. That was the drippy model with all her boyfriends who fought over taking her out in her latest outfit. Booger tucked her baton underneath her arm and got fifteen cents out of her pocket, paying the lady.

We started to walk along Stockton, heading back for the apartment house. But we happened to pass by an art shop and I stopped because there were small statues of the Eight Immortals. I pointed to a couple of the ones I couldn't name. "Who are they?" I asked Booger.

Booger had begun leafing through her comic while I looked at the window. She looked up now at where I was pointing. "Who cares." She shrugged.

"No, come on. I don't know," I said.

"Well, I don't either."

"But you can speak Chinese."

"Just because I can speak Chinese doesn't mean I'm superstitious."

"How am I being superstitious when I'm learning about my past?"

"It may be your past," she said stubbornly. "It's not mine." She looked at me angrily as if I'd just insulted her.

"Well, what is your past then? That junk?" I pointed at the comic. "All she can ever think about are boys and dresses."

Booger stiffened a little and held her comic tighter. "Don't be such a pill," she said.

I realized then that you don't have to believe in the stories. You don't even have to believe in the gods they're about; but you ought to know those stories and the gods and also know your ancestors once believed in them and tried to model their lives after certain good spirits. Booger spoke Chinese well, yet she'd cut herself off from our own rich, deep past. It was silly not to find out about it—like living on a tiny island in the ocean and being afraid to swim or fish. And I think that fear had made her into even more of an owl than me. But as soon as I realized that, I also knew that I couldn't tell it to Booger.

"Hey, nothing's wrong with the comic. Mind if I read it after you?"

"If you don't mess it up." She scurried on ahead of me like a little mouse seeing the shadow of an owl—even though she was an owl herself. It was like she was an owl who was trying to pretend to be a nice respectable mouse instead. I could hurt and scare like an owl too. But Jeanie would never have been owlish that way because she always got on so well with people. Somehow that difference between me and Jeanie made me feel kind of sad.

Chapter Four

I

THAT Monday morning around six I woke up to hear the soft *slap-slap* of the cards as Paw-Paw played at the kitchen table. The shade had been pulled up to let in what light there was on a cloudy morning. Lately it had been colder in the city. Paw-Paw was leaning forward to examine her hand.

"Good morning," she called out brightly.

I sat up in bed, pulling my knees against my chest and yawning. "Couldn't you sleep, Paw-Paw?"

Paw-Paw pistoned her arm slowly in the air. "No, my rheumatism, it kept me up."

Now that I was more awake, I could hear the pots of water bubbling in the kitchen. I wanted to be a help to her like Jeanie had been. "Why don't I light the oven, Paw-Paw?"

"No, the gas might go out and we will die." Paw-Paw sat rigidly with the pack of cards in her hand.

"I've lit stoves like that lots of times. You just hold the match to the pilot hole."

"No," she insisted, "it's too dangerous."

Maybe she had heard too many stories about people suffocating; I don't know. At any rate, she wouldn't let me argue with her. I could tell by the way she began putting the cards down so quick and so hard.

When I got dressed later that morning for school, I could see that Paw-Paw had switched from cotton slacks to wool ones and on top of everything else she had worn before, she added two more sweaters or, at other times, a vest under a padded jacket. If she had looked round before, she looked even rounder now— like a bear that had put on an extra-thick coat of fur.

Only I didn't want to have to wear so many clothes. For one thing, it was kind of bulky moving around and, for another thing, it still left my hands and face cold. I'd much rather have used the oven to heat our place up, at least in the daytime. School was warm so, even though we had to wear those drafty skirts that were part of the school uniform, I was warm. But when I got back to our place, it felt like the inside of an icebox so I changed right away to my jeans and sweat shirt and put my coat back on before I started to boil the pots of water. Paw-Paw had nothing against jeans since a Chinese woman was as likely to wear slacks as some dress.

The next few days seemed even colder. I honestly didn't know how Jeanie had stood the cold when she had lived with Paw-Paw. But maybe Jeanie had learned how to dance just to keep warm. I had to smile at that idea, and yet it was about the only good reason I could come up with for why Jeanie used to like dancing. I thought more like Barney than Jeanie. Barney had never cared much about clothes from what I'd seen in some of the old photos and as for dancing—well, maybe Barney had started hating dancing when Jeanie died. I tried to imagine what I would have been like if Jeanie had lived and helped raise me. Would I have been like her and enjoyed going to dances?

Just for the hell of it, I turned on the radio and tried to twist like I'd seen on TV once. I pretended like I was toweling myself off in back while I twisted my hips and legs, but I made the mistake of watching myself in the mirror. I looked more like a hunched monkey. "You look stupid," I told my reflection. "No. In fact, you look pathetic."

I looked at myself really hard then. Barney was right, I guess: I did look like a kangaroo when I was wearing jeans and a sweat shirt. It was funny, but Jeanie probably would have gotten on better with someone like Booger than with someone like me. It made me feel awfully lonely when I thought about it. I suppose Jeanie and me would have been okay together because from what everyone said she got along with most anybody. Even so, I would have wanted us to do more than just get along: I would have wanted her at least to be my special friend—only that would have meant being more like her.

I told myself that I was just going down to visit Booger Chew because her place was probably warm. But I don't know. I guess it was more. Maybe I was hoping that even if I couldn't get into dressing up or dancing, I could at least get along better with people, like Jeanie had.

On Saturday I went down the stairs to our landlady's apartment. The Chew family used to stay up late because the father was a partner on a farm down the peninsula where they grew flowers in gigantic hothouses to sell to the florists. He usually didn't get back until eight or nine in the evening so the whole family from the baby on used to stay up for him and have dinner together. No one got to bed till eleven and on holidays, the family stayed up even later.

So, though it was already near one, Booger was just getting up. She answered the door in a cloth robe with a lot of little animals on it.

"Hi," she said cautiously.

"Hi, you said I could look at your comic." I didn't really want to but I thought it'd be a good excuse for a visit.

"I'm . . . I'm still looking at it." She seemed reluctant to let me in.

"I'll look at it here then."

Booger stood there for a while as if she were trying to come up with some reason for not even letting me do that but she couldn't. "Okay," she finally said and stepped back so I could go in.

Sitting on the sofa in her living room was a pretty girl in a quilted bathrobe. Her hair hung down to her shoulders, where it curled up stiffly. When she moved, the hair bounced like it was a set of springs. She looked up from her physics book and mumbled a hello to me and went on munching at a giant Hershey semisweet chocolate bar.

"That's Paulette," Booger said. "She's a senior over at Lowell High. When she graduates from college, she's gonna build atom bombs the size of nickels and peddle them on the street."

Her sister, who must have been used to such comments, went right on reading. Booger led me into the back of the apartment. A set of stairs led down to a kind of little basement. Inside her room, it was all pink and frilly, like Pam-Pam's and Hedgehog's rooms. Booger even had a lamp with a frilly lampshade shining down on a little shepherdess in a hoop skirt. In some ways, this kind of room was just as strange to me as Chinatown; but I'd decided beforehand that no matter what I found in Booger's room, I'd keep my opinions to myself. Besides, when I tried to think of what my ideal bedroom would look like, I couldn't think of it because Barney and I had always spent our life moving from one cheap furnished room to another—and by furnishings I meant one wobbly dresser, two rickety chairs, a nightstand, and two twin beds.

The *Katy Keene* comic was spread open to the fashion page and beside it was a big pad of paper with clothes drawn on it. Booger moved quickly toward the drawings but I picked the pad up before Booger could put it away. She sat on a corner of her bed looking as mournful as an axe murderer who had been caught in the act. Some of the dresses looked pretty good—if you liked that kind of stuff. "I didn't know you could draw," I said.

She pulled at the ribs on her cotton bedspread. "They're only rough sketches."

"They're pretty good."

"Thanks." Booger took the pad from me and closed it. She seemed to think for a moment and then she got up and went to her bureau with the little shepherdess lamp and opened it. She took out a Pee-Chee portfolio like we had in school and opened it on her bedspread, taking out some drawings. Some of them weren't bad. She watched me anxiously while I went through them.

"I really like this one," I said. I took out a sketch of a slinky evening gown.

"That's just another rough sketch." She waved her hand at the picture as if it didn't count. But she picked it up and looked at it. "You really like it, huh?"

"Did you ever think of sending any of these sketches in to the comic?" I nodded to the Katy Keene fashion page, which contained designs submitted by the readers.

"I have, but so far they haven't used any of mine."

"Maybe they'll be in the next issue. When did you send them in? You know they put these comics out three or four months in advance."

"I guess." Booger flipped idly through the comic.

I slipped her drawings carefully into the pockets inside her Pee-Chee. "Ever think of trying to make some of your clothes from your own designs?"

"Gotta lose some weight." Booger put the folder back into her bureau drawer more carefully than she had taken it out. Then she flopped down again on her bed. "You ever see that movie *The Picture of Dorian Gray*?"

"You mean that one where the guy had a picture and he always stayed young and handsome while the picture got old and ugly?"

"Yeah, that's the one. Well, sometimes I feel like Paulette's Dorian Gray and I'm the picture. I mean, I can diet a week on just cottage cheese and lettuce while she stuffs her face every day with candy but I'll be the one who puts on five pounds." She nodded to one corner of her room, where I saw a pair of real skates—the kind with laced boots over the wheels. The white leather was cracked and worn as if they had been used a lot. "I even go out to the beach to roller-skate."

"Like it?"

"The others are so graceful and I'm so clumsy." She shrugged.

"Then why do you do it?"

"I told you it was the exercise," she said.

I didn't see where this was going to get us so I changed the subject. "Nice out at the beach?"

Her eyes went wide. "You've never been out to the beach?"

"Grandmom doesn't like to go out of Chinatown."

"It's just so neat out there. They've got this place called Playland that goes for two blocks. There's a roller coaster and a diving bell and a fun house and a whole bunch of neat games including a roller derby. And I almost always get hungry when I go out there. They've got a place that makes pronto pups—you know, that's a hot dog on a stick that's fried in cornmeal batter. Hmmm. And there's Yum-Yum. That's caramel popcorn and peanuts. There's a place for bull pups—they're really enchiladas but . . ." She went on about the food there.

I could really see why she liked to go out skating. Poor Booger, I'd give you a hundred-to-one odds that as many pounds as she lost she'd gain back before she made it to the bus to go home.

"Why do you have to look like those scrawny things?" I waved my hand at Katy Keene posing elegantly. "I bet none of them can draw half as good as you do. The faces and the scenes in your drawings are a lot more interesting than the clothes."

"I like clothes," she said defensively. "I'm not like some people who go around like bums. Why do you want to wear a sweat shirt and jeans? What have you got against dresses?"

"Well, Chinese women have been wearing slacks for a long time."

"You're an American now and women ought to wear dresses, not slacks."

"Some people would rather wear dresses of feathers than anything else in the world."

"What?" Booger looked at me like I was crazy.

I shrugged. "Clothes aren't all that important to me."

"But don't you ever want to get married? You'll never catch a man that way."

She made a husband sound like a stupid rat and herself like a piece of old, moldy cheese she had to dress up. But I didn't say that. I just shrugged again. "My grandmom does fine living by herself."

Old Boog picked at the fuzz on her bedspread as if she was trying to think that over, but it was like I was talking Martian to her. Finally, she closed her comic book.

"I got the new Beatles' single, 'Can't Buy Me Love.' Want to hear it?"

"Sure," I said.

When I got back upstairs to our apartment, I dug around in my duffel bag and got out Pam-Pam's old dress. She said that she didn't want it anymore after I had worn it. I guess I should have thrown it in their trash basket right then and there but I figured that maybe I could sell it someplace for four bits. I took off my sweat shirt and jeans and tried on the dress. It was strictly silk-purses-and-sows'-ears time.

It was stupid. Stupid. Stupid. And the thought of me trying to dance in this outfit of Pam-Pam's was so painful that I had to close my eyes. If I could have, I would have turned the mirror around so it was facing the wall and not me. I hugged myself and began to rub my hands up and down my bare arms. When I had gone down to Booger's, I had turned off the stove burners as well as the radio, so it was cold in the apartment. I suppose being in Booger's nice warm place made our place seem even colder now. I got into my jeans and then pulled my sweat shirt on over the top of the dress. And then I even tried putting on my coat. But I still felt cold.

I started to wash the rice like Paw-Paw had told me, though it took half an hour. Once I'd bought the wrong kind, getting short-grain rice when Paw-Paw liked Texas long, which she said was the closest to good Chinese rice. I had to wash it carefully, pouring it into a pot and then adding water and swirling it around with my hand, then pouring off the excess water which would turn milky from the washing. Then repeat the whole thing about a dozen times till the water I poured out was almost clear—which wasn't all that easy to see since we only had a dinky forty-watt bulb dangling from the kitchen ceiling. That way the rice never stuck.

It wasn't easy trying to be helpful like Jeanie.

Anyway, so there I was in the kitchen in practically all the clothes I had, and I still didn't feel any warmer. The water in the pots hadn't boiled yet. I had hot water coming out of the tap to warm my hands but you couldn't wash the rice for too long in hot water or it would start to cook and by the time it came off the stove it would be as mushy as that cruddy Minute rice. Though I started out using lukewarm water, it got cold fast in the frigid air and my hands got as cold as the water.

To hell with it, I thought. I could turn off the oven before she got back. So I got a book of Paw-Paw's matches and opened the oven. Then I lit a match and turned the gas on, putting the match near the little hole and hearing the soft explosion of gas igniting. Finally I twisted the gas up to three hundred fifty and went back humming to the kitchen sink to finish washing the rice.

I did that for the next few days without getting caught. Now five will get you two that I normally stay awake during the daytime. I usually never nap, but there was something that Friday about how the rainwater dripped from the fire escapes and the heat filled the place. After I had put the rice on, I started to do my homework but somehow all the little numbers began to run around on the page and I was asleep.

The next thing I knew, there was an acrid smell in the air and the banging of pots. A cloud of steam came from the kitchen. I ran to the door and saw Paw-Paw there, still in her scarf and coat, holding our cast-iron pot under the faucet. The pot was so hot that it made the water turn into steam.

I glanced at the stove. Paw-Paw had turned off both the burners and the oven. "It's . . . it's a good thing that the pot wasn't aluminum. It would have warped like crazy."

"Yes?" Paw-Paw said absently. With a big spoon she scraped the burnt rice out onto a newspaper and wrapped it up into a neat bundle. Then she set the cooling pot on the sink and reached for an S.O.S pad. In the same tight-lipped silence, she began to scrub out the burn marks from the pot, only she wasn't having too much luck.

"Did I ruin the pot, Paw-Paw?"

Paw-Paw just worked on.

"I'm real sorry." Only Paw-Paw still didn't say anything. "Aren't you going to hit me or something?"

"I don't like hitting people" was all that Paw-Paw would say. It was just like she was a stranger to me all of a sudden, like everything I knew to be my Paw-Paw had suddenly been withdrawn into a tight little shell and all that was left was this outer husk of a strange, silent, angry person.

"I wish you'd shout at me at least," I said. "This is worse than any beating."

Paw-Paw glanced at me. Then she turned her eyes back to the pot and went on scrubbing. I went back into the other room and sat down on the bed and tried to read my arithmetic book, only the numbers kept on blurring. Paw-Paw came out a moment later, wiping her hands on a dish towel. She sat down on the bed beside me. "When I came in and I saw you with your head lying on the table and the stove door open, I thought you were dead. I thought I'd lost you."

I kept my eyes on the page of the book. "Really?" I mumbled. I felt ashamed.

"Yes, really." Paw-Paw hesitated at saying any more. Like me, she didn't like to talk about her own feelings. Even so she decided to go on. "Respect differences, cherish the things you share in common." She took my hands and felt them. "But you are cold." Looking worried, she rubbed them between her warm palms. "Well, if you're sure you won't kill us or explode the stove, I guess we could light it."

"I'm not much like Jeanie," I said. "Are you disappointed?"

Paw-Paw put her arm around me and gave me a quick hug. "You can't be me. You can't be your mommy either. You can only be yourself."

"But I just keep finding out what I'm not," I complained, "never what I *am*."

"So what's wrong with that?" Paw-Paw rocked me gently. "Maybe that's how you're supposed to start. You saw me making broth. You keep taking out the bits of beef and the grease until what you have left is clear . . . the heart of the soup." She gave me a little push toward the kitchen. "Now go, light your stove."

I got up, hoping that Paw-Paw was right. I was afraid that if I kept on taking things away, I might not have anything left.

II

NEXT Monday afternoon Barney called—collect. I sat up in bed, telling the operator it was okay. "How're you doing, Barney?"

"Fine, kid. Listen, tell your Paw-Paw that I'll send her the cash to pay for this call. I'm really sorry about having to do it collect. But I didn't want you to forget what my voice sounds like."

"As if I could forget." I lay back down on the bed. "Got all your postcards. You've really been doing some traveling. I tried writing you but my letters never seem to catch up with you. The post office keeps sending them back saying you've moved already."

"Yeah." He laughed, but it sounded like a forced laugh. Barney sounded real tired and real down. "I'm kinda hard to keep up with. So don't forget to tell your Paw-Paw that I won't stick her with the bill."

"It's okay, Barney. I still got some money left that Morey loaned me. I can use that."

"That's great," Barney said, relieved. "I don't want to have your Paw-Paw pay for everything."

I tucked the receiver between my chin and left shoulder so I could put my hands behind my head. "Don't worry about it, Barney. We've been getting along just great so I don't think she'd mind."

In the background I could hear the sound of a jukebox yodeling out some country tune and voices laughing just a little too loud. I guess Barney was calling from some phone booth in a bar. "So you been having fun in Chinatown?" he asked.

"Sure. I just wish you were here to show me around this place like you did at the park."

"You gotta live your own life, baby."

"I just wish I knew what that was." I hadn't meant to say anything, but it just came out.

"Huh?"

"I mean, I'm not much like Jeanie, am I?" No matter what Paw-Paw said, that fact had been getting me real down.

"I never wanted you to be," Barney said a little sharply. "Hey, what's going on up there? Is your Paw-Paw riding you about the way you are?"

"No. No. She's been great. Honest. She said I oughta be myself. All I meant was that I didn't think I was as much of a help to you as Jeanie."

"What would you know about that?" he demanded. He sounded real uptight.

"I went into this Orange Julius the other day, see. And I got to talking to the guy behind the counter. Turns out he used to know you in high school. His name's Sheridan."

"Oh, yeah," Barney said absently as if he were trying to remember if he owed Sheridan anything.

"He said you and him had a real hard time when you got out of high school. That's all I mean."

There was silence at the other end for a while. "Well, yeah, I guess we did."

"I got pretty mad when I first heard about it. They shouldn't have treated you that way, you know? I mean, they shouldn't hold your being Chinese against you when you try to get a job."

"Well, it's done. Let's just forget it, baby. It's in the past."

"But I can't forget, Barney. It's real important to me." My voice rose a little.

"What's going on up there?" Barney sounded worried.

"Just talk to me for once about this stuff, Barney. Please."

He sighed. "It wasn't all that simple, baby," Barney explained. "There just weren't many jobs for anybody—Chinese or black or American—so naturally they kept the jobs for the American guys."

"Jeanie got a job."

"Gee-zus, Sheridan really shot off his mouth, didn't he?"

"Is that why you started gambling? Because Jeanie could get a job and you couldn't?"

"Yeah," Barney admitted reluctantly, "but I took it for ten years. And then I got smart and saw that working my ass off didn't get me anyplace." Barney paused as if he found it difficult to talk about these things. "But things were still a helluva lot better than what men like my dad had to go through. Beatings. Lynchings. You know."

"No, but I can guess. Why didn't you ever tell me about these kinda things?"

"I worry about what happens today and not what happened yesterday. Asking these kinds of questions . . ." I could hear Barney take an exasperated drag on his cigarette and then exhale. "It just makes for hard feelings again. So you should just cool it."

"There's a difference between forgiving what happened and just forgetting. You can't run away from the past. I want to know what it means to be Chinese."

"I raised you to be an American." Barney sounded annoyed.

"Well, I'm a Chinese-American then," I argued.

"Baby, you can't go around Chinatown asking a lot of questions," Barney gently scolded me. "You'll just get into trouble with the other Chinese."

"But I'm just trying to find out about what happened."

Barney's voice took on a puzzled tone. "I thought you said you're having a good time in Chinatown. Were you telling me the truth?"

"Not exactly." I wound the telephone cord around my index finger and then unwound it. "I'm getting along better than I did before, though."

"What's the matter? You too different than the others?"

"Kinda. But it's only going to be a few more months till summer, Barney. Then we'll be back together again just like always."

"I'll see what I can do about making it sooner, baby. I promise."

I clutched at the receiver. "Barney, don't do anything crazy. I can manage. Honest."

"I know you can, baby. You been carrying me all these years, so that's why I owe it to you to get you out of Chinatown as soon as I can." Barney paused. "Well, bye now."

"Barney—" I began but he had already hung up. I sat on the bed for a long time. There was no telling what Barney might do without me to watch him.

That Saturday I was sitting on the steps. Some of Paw-Paw's friends had had their social-security checks stolen right out of their mailboxes. The mailman wouldn't give me our mail because he didn't know me so I had to wait till he put all the mail in the boxes. Then I got out my key and lifted up the little door to our box and found the tan envelope with Paw-Paw's check and a plain white envelope as well that someone must have stuck in there since I got Friday's mail. I managed to pull at one loose corner of the envelope flap and rip it open. Inside was a five-dollar bill, no note. Just five dollars. I stood there puzzled for a while, but then I figured that this is what Barney must have meant when he said he'd see what he could do. I guess Barney must have one friend in San Francisco—maybe even Sheridan, for all of his acting tough—who would loan Barney the money and even bring it to me.

People like Phil didn't understand Barney. They thought he was just a lazy bum who made excuses for not working. But Barney would give you the shirt off his back if you told him you needed one for your poor brother freezing in Florida. Barney was generous to a fault and he'd always be doing crazy things like this and expect you to be just as crazy as him. I mean, he ought to have used that money to help pay Big Mike off, but he'd rather see other people happy.

I tried to think of what to use the five dollars for. Finally, I decided it'd be nice to have a good Chinese dinner. Most of the time we made do without much meat because Paw-Paw could take a quarter pound of flank steak and cut it so thin that it seemed like you were getting a lot. She'd add that to vegetables and a clove of garlic and a piece of ginger—to kill off the bugs and germs in the vegetables—and fry all of it at high heat in oil, her face intent on the steam rising, and the oil hissing and crackling. Or she could take chicken and cut it into pieces and cook it in special sauces—like one she made out of soy sauce and anise and other herbs and spices—so that you wanted to put the gravy on the rice and eat that too. You wound up filling up on rice that way rather than on meat—but Paw-Paw always grumbled that her gravies were never as good as they used to be since the stores couldn't get things from the mainland. At any rate, I thought Paw-Paw would like part of a duck like she said that time we were walking back from the movies. She wouldn't have to do so much sewing.

I went into Paw-Paw's favorite delicatessen at the upper end of Grant. It was actually a combination grocery store with fresh vegetables in crates set outside on the sidewalk. I walked down the row of crates, picking out some *bok choy* with long celerylike stems, broad leaves of a deep, almost bluish green, and little yellow flowers. The short-stemmed ones were the tenderest, Paw-Paw said. In a dry year, though, even the short stems would be tough for lack of water—or so Paw-Paw swore.

Then I went inside the store, where a counter occupied one corner. Behind the chest-high glass pane lay a row of steel pans heated by steam underneath. And each of the pans was filled with some dish: balls of ground fish and black, pungent mushrooms; cashew chicken with tender chicken breasts cut up into bite-size chunks and cashews cooked in oil so they were soft and button mushrooms and maybe baby corn—the kernels about the size of a pinhead and the whole cob as long and thick as my little finger. And skewered overhead would be slabs of barbecued spareribs waiting for the knife, or sometimes pieces of barbecued pork, their ends burnt black and tasting sweet and salty at the same time and the meat a bright red inside. Most of the time Paw-Paw just bought a little of the cheap things—stuff that she couldn't make herself or stuff that wasn't worth the bother of making for just two people.

At the moment there was only one clerk on duty, a tall, thin young man with pale skin and a round, impatient face. Paw-Paw always came to this place but she had always done the ordering—I'd just been along as a pack mule. And suddenly I realized that I didn't know much more than the names of things. I just had to hope that he spoke some English.

A lady waddled up next to me—a fat, round lady, her hair cut short and curled tightly around her head. Her pasty jowls sagged and her buckteeth, one of which was gold, showed all the time. With her bulging shopping bags in either hand, she took up enough space for three people. The clerk ladled some sliced abalone and asparagus into a cardboard container. He dipped the ladle with a languid air—like you'd expect from some rich lady reaching into her box of chocolates. And when the clerk finished with the first customer, she started rattling off an order in Chinese.

"I think I was next," I said.

The clerk glanced at me and then at the lady, tapping the tray with one of the big spoons. With his other hand he picked up an open container from the ones stacked near him. The lady went on trying to order, waving her hand imperiously at the clerk.

I tapped her arm. "Excuse me, but I think I was next."

In a loud voice, the lady started to scold me—at least I think she did, but for all I knew she might have been reciting all the names in the Hong Kong telephone directory. Then she turned to the clerk and gave him her order again. This time he grunted and began to fill up the container for her. I suppose I should have just kept my mouth shut but it was the principle of the thing—her rudeness and the clerk's willingness to go along with her—that got me.

I reached over the steel shelf at the top of the glass pane and grabbed at the clerk's arm.

"Hey, I was here before she was."

He only shrugged, pulling his arm free, and went on serving her.

At that moment a short, stocky, middle-aged man bustled over in a grease-stained tan smock. There was a little paper cap on his head and a toothpick dangled from between his teeth.

"What you want?" he asked. "I take care of you."

"I'd like half a roast duck."

"Oh-kay." He made the word sound like a song. He took a duck off a hook where it hung in the front window. Its juices had congealed on its fat, round bottom into small, white beads on the red-brown skin. He plopped that down on a cutting board to one side of the trays but still behind the glass pane. In one smooth motion he picked up a meat cleaver and brought it down with a solid meaty thwack that cut the duck's breast almost in half. Another heavy blow cut the lower part of the duck. Then he placed the cleaver along the neck and head and applied pressure gently with his fist on top of the blade, so that the bones crunched as he cut the rest of it in two. One half he laid to one side.

"*Jom ah?*" he asked.

"Excuse me?"

The young man snickered.

The man in the cap made chopping motions with his cleaver. "You want cut up?"

"Yes, please."

"How many pieces? Four? Eight?"

"Eight will be fine." I held up my fingers to be sure he understood.

It only took him a few expert cuts, the cleaver meeting the cutting board with loud *thunks* and spattering grease against the glass pane. Then he used the front of his cleaver—where the point would be on a knife—to scoop the duck into a cardboard container. On top of the pieces he ladled some juice and closed the flaps, saying something in Chinese.

I felt very self-conscious at that moment. And it didn't help any that the young man was snickering again. It must have seemed ridiculous to them that someone wouldn't know how to count out money or be able to pronounce *duck*. What I really felt like was a tourist.

"Excuse me?"

"That be one dollah and five cents," he said.

I'd made everything out to be ninety-five cents. But I figured he was adding on a dime because I couldn't speak Chinese. "It ought to be a dime less."

"Restaurant tax," the man said smoothly.

"My Paw-Paw said it was already figured into the price." I handed him the five dollars.

The young man rolled his eyes toward the ceiling while the middle-aged man muttered something. He went to a beat-up wooden cash register and banged the keys savagely. He slapped my change down on the little steel shelf on top of the glass pane. "All right. All right. I not charge sales tax then."

Well, I suppose the man had to save some face. I scooped the money into my hand and stuffed it into my pocket. "Thanks."

Still muttering to himself, the man slipped the container into a paper bag and handed it to me. I started for the street but the woman with the shopping bags was waiting for me. There was no way I could get past her. Between her bulk and her shopping bags, she filled the doorway.

"Excuse me," I said to her loudly, "I'd like to get through."

But the woman started to shout at me.

I shouted right back at her. "I'D LIKE TO GET THROUGH IF YOU'RE FINISHED."

But the woman didn't budge; she went on shouting—and not even looking at me. It was almost as if she were shouting at the world in general. Outside, people started turning their heads and even stopping to watch. I could feel the blood rushing to my face. I don't think I'd ever felt more embarrassed in my life—like one of those nightmares where you're suddenly naked in a crowd. I felt like the guilty person—not for demanding my rights but for being unable to speak Chinese so I could argue with the woman. I stood there stupidly.

At that moment the middle-aged clerk came out from behind the counter and took my arm, pulling me back into the store. "She like that. Doan mind her. Always shout. She f.o.b."

"What?"

"Fresh off the boat."

The young clerk leaned against the cash register, his arms folded, smirking broadly and enjoying the spectacle of the woman in the doorway.

The middle-aged clerk picked up an old towel and began wiping at the grease on the steel shelf. "Back in China," he explained, "all the time people they gotta push and push because things so crowded. They come over here. They doan understand they supposed wait their turn."

"Somebody ought to explain to her how things work over here," I said self-righteously.

"She go outside Chinatown, somebody have to. But in Chinatown why she need change?" The middle-aged man shrugged and I understood that I was the invader, the rude one, not her.

A lot of people lived in Chinatown because, like Paw-Paw, they wanted to. But there were a lot of people who would have liked to live away from Chinatown if they could only speak enough English. Since they couldn't, they were stuck here, paying high rents for tiny apartments, even though they might have been able to get apartments of the same size some blocks away—that's assuming that the landlords would be fair-minded and rent to Chinese, and more landlords were being fair nowadays. And those same Chinese couldn't get good-paying jobs for the same reason they couldn't move out of Chinatown so they wound up washing dishes and doing all the other dirty jobs in Chinatown and getting underpaid because they didn't even know what they ought to be earning.

It was like the Chinese were a bunch of people stuck inside a little forest grove and every day a bunch of American owls came over and dumped on them. And then one day an owl wandered into the middle of the grove and the people got a chance to get even for everything the owls ever did to them by dumping on that one owl.

Lucky for me a man in glasses came down one of the aisles.

In his hands he had a clipboard of pink inventory sheets. He flipped one of them up and began studying his shelves, making check marks by the things that needed to be reordered. "She's blocking the doorway, Jack. Get rid of her."

He must have been the owner of the store because the middle-aged clerk immediately walked back to her. He shouted at her and for a moment it was fifty-fifty who could outshout the other but since the woman had already been shouting for five minutes and was getting hoarse, the clerk won. He repeated himself again loudly and pointed at her bags. The woman immediately twisted her head to look suspiciously in either direction and said something loud, not to me, but to the crowd who had gathered behind her. She glared around at them and then waddled forward in a slow, shuffling walk, taking nothing but small half steps, and all the while she twisted her head this way and that as if she expected trouble at any moment.

"What did you tell her?" I asked him.

"I tell her she better watch bags or someone take something while she busy talking." He wiped his hands on the towel as he walked around behind the counter.

It finally hit me that even though I looked Chinese and had learned some of the myths and a little bit of the language, I'd never really fit into Chinatown the way that Jeanie had. I couldn't even be like her in being Chinese.

Trying to spend the rest of the five dollars proved just as tough—when I went to the restaurant to order some chicken chow mein, the waiter couldn't understand me too well when I said it and he brought out a carton of that crap they feed to the tourists—you know, where the noodles are fried hard and crispy like potato chips—when what I wanted was the soft, wet kind the Chinese ate. And it took a little while arguing with the waiter before he went back and got what I wanted. As I was leaving I heard him use a phrase I'd heard Mr. Jeh use: "Native-born, no brains."

And I had more trouble when I went to get some *gai bow*—those are white buns about the size of my fist in which chicken and eggs and some pieces of barbecued pork are all cooked together. I ordered four of them and held up four fingers as well.

"Nothing else?" the owner asked.

"No, that's all."

"Okay, I get them." He went into the kitchen and I could hear the voice of a woman—it probably was his wife—rise above the clanging of pots and pans. I wasn't sure but I heard him say the

Chinese word for *four* and I heard her say the word for *two*. He argued a little bit more and she said something in a sharp way. He came out looking very meek with a paper bag in his hand. "Sorry. All we got is two."

It was a small enough thing to happen and I don't mean to sound like a whiner but that day a lot of small things happened to me and they had built up inside, so that I felt like shouting as loudly as the woman and I was likely to suspect everyone. I took a chance and lied. "Just because I talk English doesn't mean I don't understand some Chinese. You've got plenty of them back there but you don't want to sell them to me unless I buy a lot of other stuff."

From the way his face flushed, I was sure I was right. He looked embarrassed and angry at the same time. "All we got is two I tell you and you're lucky to get these."

I should have known better than to call him a liar to his face. If I had asked him to count again or maybe told him I wanted them for my Paw-Paw, he might have given me what I wanted, but he needed some excuse. Now he wouldn't change his mind no matter what happened. I took the two and paid for them, feeling hot and frustrated inside and thinking that if I had ordered in Chinese, they might have given me what I wanted, or at least explained the situation to me. But to them I was an outsider.

Somehow Paw-Paw kept herself from laughing—how, I'm not sure. I know now that you order *bow* for brunch or lunch, *chow mein* for lunch, and rice and duck for dinner. It was a bit like serving up ham and eggs, a hamburger, and turkey with stuffing, all at the same time.

All Paw-Paw did when she saw the spread on the table was to stand in the middle of the room and stare. "Where did all this come from?"

So I proudly told her about the five dollars Barney had someone leave in our mailbox.

"You should have saved it," Paw-Paw scolded me good-naturedly.

"This is what Barney would have wanted." I held her coat while she slipped one arm out of a sleeve and then, half turning, slid her other arm free. "Phil said that Barney killed Jeanie because she had to hold down two jobs to try to pay off all his debts but that's not true, is it?"

"When your mommy was alive, Barney owed money because he was always generous—always loaning people money, you know. And Barney never could let anyone else pay the bill in a restaurant." Paw-Paw shook her head with a smile. "Your mommy used to get so mad at all of his friends because they would always let him."

"But Jeanie didn't blame Barney?"

"Oh, no. They argued some, especially when he started gambling, but she always loved him. She said he could never see anything bad about people and people were always taking advantage of that fact."

"Barney's really great, isn't he?"

"Yes," Paw-Paw agreed, happy for me. "Philip should be here right now." She sniffed appreciatively at the different dishes. "I was expecting leftovers." She sat down a little stiffly on her chair today because the cold damp had gotten to the rheumatism in her knees and elbows. "I can't remember when I had duck last." I brought in tea from the pot in the kitchen and set it down in the middle.

"Was it a long day at the shop?"

"Always the same. But the cloth they give us to work with gets shabbier and shabbier and some of the young ones, they don't take much care on the seams. I pity the person who buys one of the dresses they sew."

I dished some fluffy white rice into a rice bowl for Paw-Paw and then added some to a plate for myself. The steam rose from the rice, carrying a light, sweet scent. When I sat down on my stool, Paw-Paw shook her head. "Everything looks so good I don't know where to start."

"Don't just load up on rice now. *Hek soong.*" Meaning that she should eat from the side plates as well. Paw-Paw started to spoon a piece of neck onto her plate.

"No, come on, Paw-Paw." I used a serving spoon from another dish and put a meaty piece of breast on the small plate at her place.

Paw-Paw poked it with the serving spoon she had been using. "You take it."

"No, there's another meaty piece right there."

"That's the . . . the . . ." Paw-Paw hunted for the right word. "The bottom. It'll be mostly fat and that's what I like." Deftly she switched pieces. "The fat's where all the juices collect."

I picked at my piece. "You sure?"

"Of course."

I felt warm inside at being able to load the table this way with so much food. It's funny but I'd heard all those jokes about mothers who pile food onto people's plates and for the first time I felt I understood why they did that—not that I felt like getting into the hassle of cooking or wandering around in an apron; but it was nice just to be able to feed someone you liked. Only there was something incomplete about dinner and it took me a moment to realize what it was.

So maybe I couldn't be much like Jeanie had been; maybe I couldn't even be as Chinese as her. But somehow I think Jeanie would have agreed with Paw-Paw when she told me to be myself. I think Jeanie would have liked me not for imitating her but for being what I was and that meant I couldn't turn my back on being Chinese—no matter what Barney had said.

I put down my fork and went back into the kitchen to get a pair of chopsticks and a bowl. When I got back to the table, I tilted up my plate so the rice slid into the bowl.

"You don't have to do that, you know," Paw-Paw said.

My shoulders sagged a little. "Will I look too stupid?"

"Oh, no, no," Paw-Paw said. "It's just that you should be able to eat in comfort."

"I know," I said, "but I want to learn."

"Well, then." Paw-Paw picked up her chopsticks. "You have to think of the chopsticks as two long fingers growing out of your hand. You hold the bottom chopstick between these fingers." She held up her hand so I could see the chopstick was near the first joints of her middle and fourth fingers and held there rigidly. "You keep this one straight. It's the top chopstick you move around." She held the other chopstick between the tips of her thumb and index finger and she showed me how easily she moved it around. "Don't let the parts above your hand cross over and don't squeeze things either. You don't have to press too hard. That's important to remember." To show me, she lifted up the piece of duck, slippery in its own juices, from her plate and then put it back down.

I tried to lift the piece of duck from my plate. On the fourth or fifth try, I managed to lift it halfway before it fell down. Dinner was going to take a long time.

"Very good." Paw-Paw beamed. She ladled some vegetables and sauce from another bowl on top of her rice. "Now you lift your rice bowl like this." She put her thumb on the top rim of the bowl and her fingers on the bottom rim of the little base of the bowl. "That way," she explained, "you don't really feel the heat of the bowl." She lifted it up toward her mouth in her left hand. "And you put the rice into your mouth." She angled the chopsticks at the tips so they were like a little paddle and with a shoveling motion, she pushed small amounts of rice into her mouth.

"I feel just like a kid again," I said apologetically. "I mean, I have to learn how to eat all over again." When I tried to use the chopsticks, I felt as awkward as if my fingers were an owl's talons. Paw-Paw did not laugh at me—even though dinner took twice as long as usual.

Afterwards, while we were doing the dishes, I glanced over at Paw-Paw, who wore an apron of green on a bright red background. "Paw-Paw, what's my name?"

"You know your name, girl."

"No, I mean my Chinese name."

"She came to me on her . . . let me see." Paw-Paw looked at the wall for a moment. "Yes, on her thirty-fifth birthday, to tell me the news. I was so surprised. And she told me, 'Mama, pick out the prettiest name you can. I won't pick out an American name until she has her Chinese name.' That's what she said."

"How did she know to pick out a girl's name?"

Paw-Paw shrugged matter-of-factly. "I held the charm to her stomach and it turned in the way it should for a girl."

"Well, what's my name?"

"*Cheun Meih*," Paw-Paw said. When she said the words, they didn't sound like funny noises anymore. They sounded a little like singing. "It means Taste of Spring."

"Teach me how to say my name."

"Yes, of course." And we practiced it until I could sing my own name. My first name. My real name. My true name.

Chapter Five

April 1965

THE next eight months went quickly—it seemed like I had lived most of my life with Paw-Paw instead of less than a year. I learned some Chinese, thanks to Paw-Paw and Booger, and at least managed to scrape by in Chinese school; and when I went shopping, I could get what I wanted, even if I didn't speak grammatically. Before I knew it, it got to be Easter already.

Because I went to a Catholic school, my vacation started on Easter weekend and went on through the next so I was home the day after Easter to check on the mail. I got another one of Barney's postcards, this one of a purple-and-yellow motel somewhere at the bottom of the San Joaquin valley. The last few months Barney had tried his luck out in L.A. and San Diego. I suppose Barney was starting to make his way back up north, trying to do some picking. But there was no telling where Barney was now since the postmark on his card showed it had been mailed some ten days ago. There was also a letter I'd written to his last address. I still hadn't connected with him yet.

"A postcard from your daddy?" Paw-Paw asked when I came in.

"Yes." I held the postcard out for Paw-Paw to see.

She leaned forward away from her chair, peering at it in a friendly way. "Look at what a pretty house."

"Yeah, I guess." I ducked under the bed and got out the two wooden cigar boxes that Mr. Jeh had gotten for me. The restaurant where he worked had a counter that sold cigars so he could always pick up the empty boxes. At these times, Paw-Paw always found something to do. Right then, she went back to fiddling around with the catch on the necklace of the charm, every now and then muttering to herself in Chinese—the kind of Chinese she used sometimes and would never translate for me. I opened the one box that had all of Barney's postcards, no two of them from the same place. I read through Barney's latest postcard:

Baby,
  My luck's still slow. Hope you're not too down. Only two months to go and then we'll show them.

Barney

I riffled through the other postcards. Barney had written pretty much the same thing on each of his postcards for the last eight months. He was always worrying about me left behind in China-town and always counting off the time till we'd be back together. I added Barney's latest postcard to my collection.

Then I took the other cigar box and put it on my lap. Inside I had all of the letters that I'd sent to Barney and that had been returned with the same stamped message on it: *ADDRESSEE MOVED. NO FORWARDING ADDRESS.* I added that letter to the bunch of letters there. I figured I'd give them all to Barney once we got back together. Then he could see what my year had been like because I wrote the letters kind of like you'd keep the pages of a diary, only I always added a paragraph trying to tell him that things were a lot better for me since we'd last talked on the phone and that I was getting on better in Chinatown and with people. If Barney could get one of my letters, maybe he'd stop worrying about me.

And maybe he could tell his friend to stop leaving money for me, because the five dollars in a plain envelope came regularly every Friday—I told Barney in every letter to stop the loans. I didn't see how he could ever pay off Barney's friend and Big Mike too. But maybe Barney had done some fast talking to that friend of his or maybe the friend had remembered how generous Barney could be when he did have a little money or maybe one of those guys who had cheated Barney just felt guilty.

I dropped the lid shut on the letter box and stowed both of them away underneath the bed.

Paw-Paw opened up her coin purse with a snap. I sat up to see Paw-Paw count out the coins she had spilled into her palm. "I think we have just enough for a movie."

"Two movies in the same month, Paw-Paw?"

She closed her fist over the coins and smiled. "Why not? Did they make a new law against enjoying yourself?"

"What about the catch on the necklace? You oughta use the money to get the catch fixed."

"I can sew more dresses this week."

But lately her eyes weren't what they used to be, which is why she stayed home more. "You've been getting an awful lot of headaches lately."

"It's nothing. That special tea Mr. Jeh gave me will cure that. Then you watch those dresses fly from my machine." She put the charm in her favorite red scarf and wrapped it up. "Besides, this old rock is too heavy to wear today."

This time when we reached the movie theater, I took out some of the money Barney had been sending me. I got to the ticket office first and held up two fingers, pointing at Paw-Paw and then at me. Paw-Paw didn't enjoy the movie too much. And we didn't take our usual leisurely walk down Grant Avenue either. Instead Paw-Paw hurried on. I saw that I'd hurt her pride.

Even though she lived on such a tight budget, she always put some aside to buy small presents for all of her grandchildren—and she had a lot of those—as well as for her children. And any of her relatives who came to visit her got some silver. Even Phil the Pill got a dollar each week he came to her apartment—sometimes it was a silver dollar she had saved, other times it was two fifty-cent pieces or four quarters. Phil had long since stopped arguing with her, pocketing the money that she pushed into his hand. Neither of them was supposed to look at the exchange taking place or call attention to it with words. That would have made Phil seem greedy, Paw-Paw told me when I had asked her about that once.

"Paw-Paw, the money came out of Barney's money. I had some left from buying dinner this week."

"He sent that money to you. You should have bought something for yourself," Paw-Paw insisted. "Like milk or candy."

"Why can't we spend it together?"

"Because I don't need to spend money on myself. I've seen everything I've wanted to see and done everything I've wanted to do so it's just a waste to spend money on an old woman."

I took her by her arm. "You're not old, Paw-Paw."

She patted my hand. "You little liar." But she seemed more comfortable.

We took our time going up Clay, cutting across to Sacramento by the little alley that ran above the playground. They'd put down some new tanbark by the swings so it stank like a whole bunch of cow patties freshly laid and the whole place was deserted. We took our time jaywalking across Sacramento—like some of the older Chinese, Paw-Paw took it matter-of-factly that any driver would respect her years and slam on the brakes in time. For those old Chinese the crosswalks and traffic lights meant nothing.

When we were in the alley, we could hear The Beach Boys and Paw-Paw started humming. She always kept the radio and one light on to fool burglars. She fished a hand in her pocket and got out her keys. She kept them separate from her purse, on an old, worn leather key chain that Jeanie had given her. There were fifty-two steps from the stoop of the apartment house up the three flights of stairs to Paw-Paw's room. She counted them several times a day seven days a week, laboring up them.

Paw-Paw was just putting her key to the lock, when she cocked her head to one side and listened.

"What—" I began.

Paw-Paw put a finger to her lips. I listened too and through the melody of "Alley Oop," I could hear the jingling sound. Somebody must have found the drawer where Paw-Paw kept her silver money. Paw-Paw slipped the key into the lock and she put her hand on the doorknob.

I put my hand on her wrist. "No, Paw-Paw. You can't have more than four dollars of silver money in there. And you could get hurt."

Paw-Paw took her hand off the doorknob and started to rub her neck the way she did when she was thinking. She stopped, frightened.

"The charm," she whispered.

"Don't go in, Paw-Paw."

But Paw-Paw turned determinedly to the door. With her left hand she twisted the key in the special lock above the door and with her right hand she turned the doorknob, pushing the door open. I tried to pull Paw-Paw back but she bulled her way in. It was a cloudy afternoon so it was dark inside her little room but I could see the figure silhouetted against the light from the window. It was like some blob had risen up from a pool of black tar inside the room.

Paw-Paw swung her purse above her head. "Stop, thief. Stop."

And now she was inside the room, silhouetted against the window like she was a shadow figure herself. She beat at the thief with her purse so hard that it flew out of her hand, crashing somewhere inside the room. The shadow figure had turned to the window and Paw-Paw threw herself at him. For a moment the thief thrashed around, pulling Paw-Paw first to the left, then to the right—like she had caught too big a fish.

"Paw-Paw, let him go."

My voice seemed to act like a whip. Up until now the thief had kept his face turned to the window, but now he wheeled around and swung his fist up. In the meantime, Paw-Paw had frozen on his arm, staring at the face only she could see. Then the thief's fist smashed into her jaw. Paw-Paw fell back, slamming against the bureau so that the statues rattled.

"Paw-Paw," I said. My eyes were on the still figure of Paw-Paw lying on the floor rather than on the thief as he slipped through the window and down the fire escape. Trembling, my hands found the light switch. Paw-Paw lay on her side, her leg against the bureau. I knelt beside her. "Paw-Paw, are you all right?"

"I fell against the bureau." Paw-Paw started to sit up and winced.

She put one hand down to her leg. "That stupid old bone in my leg, I think it's broken. Just from a little fall." She tried to give a little laugh. "Can you imagine that?"

We had to get an ambulance to take Paw-Paw to Chinese Hospital. They wouldn't let me past the lobby. This fat, efficient nurse looked down at me and told me children were not allowed because we carried germs. It didn't do any good to tell her that I sponge-bathed every day and to the best of my knowledge I'd never given anyone the Black Death, let alone dandruff. I had to fill out forms and by the time I was finished, this young Chinese doctor came out to tell me broken bones can be serious when you're older but that I wasn't to worry yet.

The hospital was too tiny to try sneaking up to see Paw-Paw the way I had when Barney was hurt, so I walked the half mile back home and started making phone calls. I tried the motel on the last postcard Barney had sent but like I thought he had already checked out of the place. Then I phoned my uncles and aunt from Paw-Paw's phone book—it was all written in Phil's meticulous hand. When I was finished making the calls, I just sat on the bed with my back to the wall, feeling real tired inside and watching the day end and the streetlamp come on outside that damned window the thief had come through.

Word spreads fast in Chinatown, especially if there's any bad luck or juicy gossip involved. It wasn't more than two hours before Booger knocked. With her foot she dragged the stool over to the side of the bed and sat down by me.

I found my jacket and took out the candy bar in the pocket. "Want some Turkish Taffy?"

Booger craned her neck forward. "What flavor is it?"

"Chocolate."

"Okay."

I took the candy bar and cracked it hard against the headboard. Then I tore open the wrapper so that we could pick up the pieces. Booger fished around in the fragments.

"Mom wants you to come down to have dinner with us."

I didn't much feel like going down to Booger's place, not that Booger's mom was a bad cook. It was just that their apartment was so neat and tidy with lace doilies over the sofas and chairs and her husband and Booger and all her family looked so scrubbed. Whenever I was down there, I felt like photographers from *Ladies' Home Journal* were going to break down the door any moment and take pictures. I felt out of place in their living room.

"Thanks, but you guys eat too late." That was the truth.

Booger stopped with a piece of chocolate halfway to her mouth. "This isn't your dinner, is it?"

"Of course not," I lied. "This is just a snack."

"Well, when are you going to cook dinner?"

The doorbell stopped Booger's third degree. It turned out to be Phil. I'll give this much to Phil, he came down right away—couldn't wait to make a big nuisance of himself I guess. He plopped his hat down on the bed and, pinching the material of his pants around the knees, pulled them up a little so he could squat. He studied the bureau.

Booger and I watched curiously. Finally he straightened, smoothing out his pants. "Well, it beats me how she could fall right there and hurt herself on the bureau. It isn't like her to be that clumsy."

For some reason Paw-Paw didn't want to call the police. I figured it was better to humor her while she was in the hospital and not tell Phil anything. I figured the charm wasn't as easy to fence as some toaster or TV. It'd take time for the thief to find somebody else to sell it to.

Only Phil took it all out on poor Booger, saying it was her great-aunt's fault for not lighting the apartments better and for putting slippery linoleum over the floor instead of carpets. I looked at the clock. "Hey, Booger, didn't you have to be home at seven?" I lied.

"What? Oh, yeah." Booger twisted around and looked at the clock. "Jeez. I'm late." She grabbed her coat, glad of the excuse. "Hey, Case, you come by anytime you want. We always got plenty of stuff in the icebox."

"Yeah, thanks. Bye." I held the door open for her while Booger made her escape, taking the steps two at a time. By the time I closed the door, Phil had already slunk into the kitchen to poke around.

"You sure you got enough to eat?" Phil the Pill went around slamming the cabinet and refrigerator doors. He sounded doubtful. I suppose *he* could have gone through everything there in one meal.

"Yea, sure." I set the cards down one by one. *Slap. Slap. Slap.*

Phil stood in the doorway and he ran his hand through his hair. "Casey, maybe you better come live with us again." He looked like he meant it. "I know we haven't always gotten along in the past, but . . ."

"I want to be near Paw-Paw." I shrugged.

"What for? You can't go up to see her anyway."

"Thanks, but I'm staying." Somehow I didn't see myself with Pam-Pam again. I mean, my God, the only card game she knew was Old Maid.

"It'd make things a lot easier for me, Casey. Then I wouldn't have to check on you and on Mother."

"I got her to the hospital, didn't I?"

"Ambulances cost fifty dollars. How can you pay for that?"

"I'll sell pencils."

"Don't be flip with me, young lady."

"I'm not young. Sometimes I feel sixty years old."

Phil sighed. He turned and with one hand opened the lock and with the other turned the doorknob. "I'll check on you tomorrow."

I just slapped the cards down. It didn't seem to sink into Phil's mind that the last thing in the world I wanted was his help.

When he opened the door, though, I could hear voices coming up the stairs.

"You're going too fast," said an old, deep voice.

"Hey, Uncle, this stairway's only big enough for one of us. I gotta go on ahead of you one step."

I walked outside with Phil and looked over the banister and saw Gilbert the Pachinko and Mr. Jeh coming up the stairs. The Pachinko was going on ahead one step at a time, trying to help Mr. Jeh up though his great-uncle kept on insisting he didn't need any help.

"Them," Phil muttered.

"What's wrong with *them*?" I demanded.

"The young one is going to the electric chair while the old one thinks that electricity is only a passing fad."

I ignored that. "Hey." I leaned over the banister and waved at them. "Hey, I'm up here."

It took them about five minutes to make it up the stairs—most of that time was spent in arguing with each other. When they finally reached the landing, Mr. Jeh snorted at Phil. "You going, yes or no?"

Phil opened and shut his mouth. In his own way, Phil wasn't a bad guy, just dense. "You couldn't pay me to stay," he said. He jammed his Gregory Peckish hat on his head and gave a tug to his impeccably Gregory Peckish coat and started down the stairs, almost skipping along like a mountain goat.

Mr. Jeh sat down inside our place, getting his breath back while he fanned himself with an old Chinese newspaper. The Pachinko seemed to be as much out of breath as his great-uncle because he had kept on talking to the old man all the way up the stairs, but he still had some wind left. "We came as soon as we heard," the Pachinko said.

Surprised, I stopped bolting the door, because I could understand what the Pachinko had said. Now that he didn't have an audience around, he was speaking clearly enunciated English. He was standing up fairly straight too.

"How's Paw-Paw?" I asked.

"She giving the nurses a hard time," Mr. Jeh said. "I expect that. The only real problem she got is worrying about you. She ask us check on you."

"I'm okay." I shrugged. "I'm used to taking care of myself."

"Well, I guess we tell her you're doing fine except for worrying about her," the Pachinko said.

"The rest of the club up there," Mr. Jeh said. "It look like a convention, you bet."

"At least she's not by herself."

"I thought Barney'd be either over there or here." The Pachinko was looking around thoughtfully.

"How would I get hold of him?" I said, annoyed. The Pachinko looked surprised. I didn't see that it was any of his business, though, what Barney did. I went into the kitchen and got a pan out of the cabinet and turned on the tap. The water rang hollowly against the pan's bottom. "Want some tea?"

"That be good now," Mr. Jeh said. The Pachinko was standing by the window when I came out after putting the water on to boil.

"See." The Pachinko was pointing to the clasp on the window. "This is where he used his knife or something to move the clasp over. You can see the scratch marks."

"You know what happened?" I asked.

"The old lady told us," the Pachinko said.

"She tell me," Mr. Jeh corrected his grandnephew. "You happen be there and overhear. If I know your Chinese that good, I send you out of room, you bet. You should have manners go out by yourself." Mr. Jeh sounded very stern.

The Pachinko took out a cigarette and tapped it against the

wall. He kept his voice level. "If I had gone out, you would have scolded me for being so impatient."

Mr. Jeh sucked at his lips thoughtfully for a moment and then grunted. "Maybe yes. Maybe no." He sighed. "Well, boy, you tell me. One of your no-good friends take it, or not?"

The Pachinko didn't change his expression at all. Casually he struck a match one-handed and lit his cigarette. "None of my friends would have wanted to take her charm, Uncle."

"No lie to me, boy," Mr. Jeh said. "You bring back now, no questions asked."

I don't know. Maybe the Pachinko had had his friends accused of other crimes like this a lot of times before because he acted real cool, just like his great-uncle was asking him about the weather. But it seemed awfully funny to me that he didn't get mad at being accused that way. It was almost like he couldn't get mad because he knew his great-uncle was telling the truth.

All the Pachinko did was glance at his gold Swiss watch. "If you won't be needing me, Uncle, I'll go and do some errands."

Mr. Jeh snorted. "Like sell charm."

The Pachinko snuffed out his cigarette in Paw-Paw's ashtray. "Just things," he said evasively. I opened the door for him and he left. Then I went into the kitchen and put the hot water and the tea into the teapot. Mr. Jeh was sitting by the table, looking out the window. Through the bars on the floor of the fire escape, he could just make out his grandnephew's back turning the corner of the lamplit alley.

I sat down on the stool, lifting the lid of the teapot to check on the steeping. The liquid was already a clear amber so I put the lid back and poured out the tea into two cups. Mr. Jeh accepted his with a nod of thanks but he sipped it without seeming to taste it.

"You know why your Paw-Paw, she not want us to go to police?"

"I think she saw his face when they were wrestling, but when I asked her in the ambulance if she had, she said no."

And looking outside at the alley, I could feel something stirring inside me—maybe like an owl waking up before it went hunting. It was a kind of nervous waiting.

"I think she know thief. She not like to hurt her friends. She maybe hope to take care of it on her own when she get out." Mr. Jeh set his cup down firmly. "Gilbert not really bad boy," he gruffed. "Just wild. No discipline at home. Too much to eat, plenty of clothes, plenty warm home. Take everything for granted and always want more, more. I feel great shame." Having come to some decision, Mr. Jeh slowly pushed himself up from the chair. His shoulders and arms were still strong and limber even if his legs had turned thin and brittle despite all the exercise he gave them. "Many thanks for the tea. I go now. I got some visits to make."

"Please, Mr. Jeh, where are you going?"

Mr. Jeh hesitated for a moment. "I go out, talk to some people I know."

"I'm coming too."

Mr. Jeh thought about that for a moment. "You no talk unless I tell you you can?"

"I'll be quiet, honest."

"All right. You got right to be along. She your Ah-Paw."

We took our time going down the steep hillside. From the church across the street I could hear the hymns begin to rise. We waited until the traffic cleared on the narrow, one-way street. Then we crossed over to the mouth of Waverly, which was an alley running two blocks through the heart of Chinatown. There wasn't much to it except a newspaper office, the back gate to the playground, some churches, and barbershops. Mr. Jeh smiled and nodded up the street. "This used be some place, you bet."

"This place?" I didn't see anything very special about it.

He shook his head. "You not judge by what you see now. Before earthquake and fire, this used be some tough, fun place. All Tong men used come here, and there be some gambling games going on and girls singing. You bet. My father used take me here all time when I was boy. I was always full of curiosity about this place. Almost all men in Chinatown. Very few women. Most of these used sell themselves."

He glanced at me and stopped, embarrassed. But I'd met hookers before because sometimes Barney and me stayed in a hotel that some hookers might be using for business and not residential purposes. The hookers hadn't just been Chinese either but most every race.

"I know about hookers," I said.

"These girls had no hooks." He looked a little puzzled. Mr. Jeh wasn't up on all the recent slang in English. "You have to understand. Most men no can bring their wives over here because the 'Mericans not let them so they find fun where can."

"And the girls?"

"It not easy at all for them," he admitted.

We walked along in silence, Mr. Jeh in his memories and I in my thoughts. While he was with me I felt as if the Chinatown I saw at that moment was only the reflection on a pool and Mr. Jeh was the breeze that moved across the still waters, making the reflection shimmer and become unreal so that I could sense the other Chinatowns of the past that lay within the dark depths.

"Listen." Mr. Jeh tilted his head to one side as if straining to hear. I guess I only imagined it but it was almost like I could see the men moving like large, black fish through the dimly lit streets and hear the voices—ever so faint, ever so distant—of the girls trying to sound happy, trying to laugh, trying to sing. And at that moment I truly felt like a child of the owl floating through a world in which the living rubbed shoulders with the dead, and the ghosts of heroes long passed on wondered over the transistor radios in the store windows.

We stopped by a Laundromat in the middle of Waverly. Mr. Jeh jingled the money in his pockets. "I feel lucky today," he said. "We see Mr. Fong."

Mr. Fong was a short, fat, balding man inside, pushing a mop in front of him in a very bored way. He seemed to be rearranging the dirt on the floor rather than wiping it up. He smiled when he saw Mr. Jeh and said something in Chinese to him.

Mr. Jeh glanced at me. "I want practice my 'Merican."

Mr. Fong shrugged. "Suit yourself. How'd you know I just got in my new lottery tickets? Very lucky." He leaned his mop against the wall and went into the back, bringing an old wooden cigar box out of a closet there. When he lifted the lid, I saw, bound up in a rubber band, a packet of sheets with Chinese characters on them. He slipped one of the sheets out and handed it to Mr. Jeh.

Mr. Jeh waved the paper at me. "You look at one of oldest things in Chinatown. My father used buy tickets from his father."

"Your father was too lucky. He nearly broke the company a couple of times," Mr. Fong agreed. "Too bad he sent all his money home."

"Bought big, fancy house but that gone now. All things gone," Mr. Jeh said.

"Fancy house," Mr. Fong said contemptuously. "We had a whole mountain of iron, another mountain of coal, and a small railroad. Used to get free rides."

"The only free rides you get on the back of a water buffalo."

Mr. Jeh laughed. Mr. Fong shrugged goodnaturedly.

"A fancy house or a railroad, who can tell now what's a lie about the past?"

Mr. Jeh went back to studying the lottery ticket rather than argue with his friend. "You know, I bet these tickets old even back in China."

"Maybe," nodded his friend. "There are some Chinese born with dice in their hands."

"Yes, well," Mr. Jeh said hastily. He glanced at me. "You help me pick out five lucky words."

"I can't read Chinese," I confessed.

"All better. You pick words by their lucky feeling. You pick out five words and they pay you so much back. You get four out of five, you get less, and so on."

"What's the lucky feeling?"

Mr. Jeh looked helplessly at his friend for a moment and then back to me. "It's when you feel good and rich and you're sure everything's right about the world. Here." He turned me to the picture of the fat little man in mandarin robes and cap that was taped to the back wall. "Ask the god of money to help you."

The picture on the wall was like the one Paw-Paw had in her place and like the pictures I had seen all over Chinatown: in delicatessens, in sewing-machine shops, in souvenir shops, even in restaurants. Paw-Paw had once tried to explain the god by saying he was a god of *fat choy*—good luck. Remembering the stories of how poor she was in China, I suppose riches meant the same thing as good luck.

I stared at the picture, not feeling like I could pray to a god I didn't really know. Then I went over the sheet and picked out four words quickly. And then a fifth. As quickly as I pointed to them, the bald man circled them with a stubby pencil. When I was finished, he took the sheet from me. "How much?" he asked.

Mr. Jeh felt in his pocket thoughtfully. "Fifty cents."

Mr. Fong sighed. "Even if you get all five words, you'll never get rich that way." He picked up the fifty cents and put it in the cigar box along with the lottery ticket.

"I have only small, small luck," Mr. Jeh said, "so I no can risk using it up by betting big."

"You'll never get rich," Mr. Fong insisted. "And you've got plenty of luck."

"Now I know someone who got luck she not use up."

"You mean the Owl Lady?"

"She's Ah Low," snapped Mr. Jeh.

"Yes, of course," Mr. Fong agreed quickly.

"I hear her charm, it might be misplaced. Maybe someone find and try and sell."

"Who'd buy it?" Mr. Fong shook his head. "Oh, it's valuable, but it'd be so shameful. Shameful."

"Yes, it be shame to buy it." Mr. Jeh picked up a back scratcher, twirling it casually between his fingers. "It might even be bad luck for them."

Mr. Fong's eyes narrowed ever so slightly. "How so?"

"She has friends who not take that kindly. And her son, he a rich, famous lawyer with many friends on the police force. Some policemens, they can be very, very mean to store owners—and what store owner not have a few things wrong with his shop the way they make so many, many laws today? Maybe a lid loose on garbage can. Maybe wire fence cover up back alleyway."

Mr. Fong put away the box. His manner became very brusque. "Yes, well, it must be nice to have such powerful friends and relatives. I'm only a lonely old man after all."

We started down the aisle between the machines. "Why did—" I began, but Mr. Jeh shook his head sharply and I held my peace until we had stepped outside into the alley.

"What were you talking about?"

"He's one of the biggest fences in Chinatown."

"Him?"

Mr. Jeh nodded. "You go into back of his place, you find it full of televisions and radios, you bet. He give other store owners bad name." Mr. Jeh chuckled as he remembered something. "I know one poor man. His set stolen so he went to Fong to buy new one. Fong, he try to bring out this set and try and sell him. But that same set stolen from man."

"What happened?"

"Fong gave it back him with some money so he keep quiet. And then when man's radio stolen, he go to Fong again, but when Fong see him, he hold up his hands and he say, 'Oh, no, not me. My friends only steal from 'Mericans now.' "

"Would they bring something like the charm to him?"

"No, but he spread word to others. He a good man really. He pay for big funeral of his great-uncle and he put four kids through college. But he make one become doctor; just in case some customer beat him up, he get free care."

We walked on down toward Grant Avenue and I saw the usual crowd of tourists and shoppers on the street. Mr. Jeh stopped by a dim little restaurant for a moment on one side of Grant. There was a menu written only in Chinese that was taped to the window. Inside the tables were hidden by wooden booths with mostly old Chinese men and women going in and out. "It was the day we found out the Manchus had been chased out of China and they declare Republic. It was restaurant then too and my father's favorite place for lunch. Suddenly this man, he stood up and shout 'Up Revolution' and he start sawing off his queue with his penknife. And then someone run into kitchen and he come out with whole bunch of knives and pass them around so everyone can cut off her queue." Chinese doesn't make any distinction about sex in the personal pronoun so people like Mr. Jeh would sometimes get the gender confused. "But the restaurant owner, he think his queue make him look handsome and he not want to cut his off even when we tell him it only make him look like dog of slave."

"What did you do then?" I asked.

Mr. Jeh chuckled. "We pick him up kicking and screaming and carry him out and give him free haircut." He shook his head. "The air thick with the smell of gunpowder from all firecrackers going off, and ground, it covered with all little bits of red paper—like red snow. And whole street filled with queues that men cut off and the queues, they lie around like a whole bunch of black snakes." He blinked and looked around vaguely as if he had to realize where he was again. "But that over fifty years ago."

But it almost seemed like I could hear, among the sharp banging of the firecrackers, the *flop-flop-flop* of long, heavy queues dropping to the ground. And as we walked on, Mr. Jeh pointed out other spots in Chinatown that reached back into the past, and some of these memories were stained with blood— like the sites of battles among the brotherhoods, or places filled with dreams where Sun Yatsen stayed to speak of revolutions.

He crossed Grant Avenue abruptly, ignoring the Ford pickup truck that honked at him angrily. It was as if he wanted to leave those thoughts behind him. We threaded our way through the tourists for a block or so until we came to a four-story building with a fake Chinese roof at the top. There was only part of a roof attached to the stone front, but this curled outwards and up like the roofs you see on pagodas. And on the fourth floor there was a kind of balcony with an iron fence and pillars, all of them done in stylized, abstract Chinese words or animal or flower designs. The entire building was painted the brightest green and red that money could buy. It was like the person who had built the place couldn't make up his mind if he wanted an American or Chinese one.

A store occupied the bottom floor. The shelves in its windows were jammed with art objects without any try at display. Just a set of shelves in the window on which the statues and vases stood. But they were more than statues.

I saw the Eight Immortals, looking as if they were ready to gather at some wine shop for a drink together or set off on some adventure. But right in the middle of the Eight Immortals stood the god of war, his face all bloody, looking ready to leap out and brandish his spear. And there were also delicate porcelain flowers or white vases, cool as iced light, and cute rabbits and deer scattered without any rhyme or reason among the statues of the gods and heroes and saints. The way that the statues were dumped on the shelves, they seemed more like cans of soup than the special things they were.

"Look at that fool," growled Mr. Jeh. "He put god of war in middle of Eight Immortals. He know better than that. He just not care. Like time he take big, beautiful statue of Buddha-to-be and sell to fancy 'Merican store so they could put it in window with dummies in furs. The fool is my *jat*."

"Pardon?"

"*Jat* is brother's son. There a different word for sister's son. His daughter work in store with him."

"Do you have a word for her too?"

"Yes, *jaht-syun-neui*, for female child of your brother's son. But you might as well call them know-nothings."

A pretty girl paused in the middle of dusting a set of shelves and smiled when she saw us opening the door. "Uncle, what are you doing here?"

Mr. Jeh took off his hat and his expression softened a little. "Nice see you, Mabel. This my friend Casey. Your father, is he in?"

"He should be home resting but you know how Dad is."

"That man, he not be happy till he get every dollar in world."

Mabel laughed. "Come on." She led us around to the back to a tiny office in which a desk and tall filing cabinet had been jammed. Everything was covered with stacks of art catalogues, orders, and books, and an electric fan perched precariously on a swaying pile of books and papers. A man, as fat as Mr. Jeh was thin, sat in the middle of a big office chair on casters. It was strange but you could see they were related after all—it was like seeing Mr. Jeh fifty pounds heavier.

"Uncle," the fat man said, "for God's sake." He was chewing on a huge cigar and he took it out now as he tried to heave himself out of his chair.

"Not try, Sherman. You may not get back into chair again."

Sherman let out a big booming laugh that seemed too much for the small room to hold. Mabel brought in two folding chairs and somehow opened them in the office and found space for them so we could sit down.

"I thought the doctor tell you not to smoke, Sherman." Mr. Jeh nodded to the cigar.

"Yeah, but I'm so used to having the damn things in my mouth that I put 'em there anyway and chew on 'em. But I guess you wouldn't know about vices." Sherman shook his head. "Damn, but you're looking even better, Uncle. I think you're going to outlive us all."

"You not speak like that," Mr. Jeh warned. "Some demon, he pass by and hear and then big trouble for me."

"Sure, sure. Sorry, Uncle. I keep forgetting." Sherman winked at me. "Got time for a snack? It may be the last time you'll see this fat nephew of yours alive."

Sherman got the appropriate reaction from Mr. Jeh, which is what Sherman seemed to want. And even as his uncle was scolding him, Sherman was already telling Mabel to go to the restaurant next door. We heard the bell on the door ring as she left. She returned a moment later with a large pink box filled with enough meat pastries and *bow* to feed an army.

"There's a new cook over there, Uncle. You ought to try his stuff."

"This stuff is for lunch, but it evening now," Mr. Jeh said, bristling with disapproval.

"It's just a snack," his nephew said good-humoredly.

"When it time for lunch, I eat lunch. When it time for dinner, I eat dinner." Mr. Jeh turned to me. "But you help yourself."

Sherman went on eating. "Funny, this must be my day for visitors. Sheridan's kid, Gilbert, was just in."

"Oh?" Mr. Jeh tried to keep his voice pitched casually.

Sherman wiped his greasy fingers on a napkin, balling it up. Then he spread a new napkin across his lap—or as much as he could cover of his large lap with the tiny paper napkin—and reached for a handful of meat pastries to pop into his mouth. "Yes, he wanted to know what legitimate art dealers might have small conscience about buying an art object of . . . well . . . suspect pedigree."

"Boys, they get curious about funniest things," Mr. Jeh said carefully.

"Yes, that's what I thought," Sherman said.

Mr. Jeh added with equal care, "You remember my friend Ah Low?"

"Yes, the one with the old owl charm."

"We think it stolen."

"You think?"

"She not talk. Maybe not want hurt friends."

There was some silent exchange between the two of them as if they both suspected Gilbert and were determined to do the right thing by Paw-Paw and yet protect their own family's honor.

Finally Mr. Jeh spoke. "I thought maybe you tell other art dealers—"

"Certainly. Certainly," Sherman said smoothly and picked up a pen in his greasy fingers and made a quick note on a pad. "I'll give them all a ring as soon as I finish."

Mr. Jeh looked around at the pink box. "By time you finish snack and dinner, it be midnight."

"All the more reason for you to pitch in. Gotta get something into you, Uncle, somehow." He waved a hand at me. "Come on, sticks and bones, you'll blow away in the first wind."

It was around nine before Sherman would let us leave. In my pocket I had a pack of a dozen plastic, imitation ivory chopsticks—a parting gift from him.

"We not find your charm today," Mr. Jeh said, "but maybe we start things so that we will. By tonight Sherman spread word among all legitimate dealers."

"Well, at least we had lunch . . . I mean, dinner."

"The Chinese, they may forget their history. They forget all old stories. They may even forget how talk their own language. But they never forget how to make money and how to eat, you bet."

I turned back to look at the store for a moment, feeling some satisfaction that I could at least recognize some of the things in the window there. And that was when I saw the Listener—the one who refused to enter heaven until everyone else was saved—over in one corner on the lowest shelf. The statue was a small one and since it was surrounded by bright green-and-blue ceramic parakeets, it was easy to miss. The Listener was fine, white porcelain and made as if she were sitting with a lotus in her hand, but it was her smile that got me. It was a smile of longing, a smile of sadness, a knowing smile, a patient smile. It must have been the way the Owl Spirit smiled. I leaned closer to look at her better and saw my reflection on the window, floating ghostlike around the solid statue with the reflection of the neon signs—as if my face were turning into a mist of lights surrounding the statue. And the smile of the statue—the smile of the Owl Spirit—was the smile on my own face.

Chapter Six

THAT night I dreamt of floating above the world, my arms spread out and the flesh of my hand silver in the moonlight. And I saw then that my fingers curled inwards toward the palms and I could not straighten my fingers no matter how much I tried. And it was like my fingernails had grown down over and around my fingers so they were shut up in shining, smooth, casings, hard and sharp as talons. I drifted gently beneath the moon through the night sky, listening as the earth and woods whispered up to me. And slipping down beside the banks of a stream I saw another creature of the night, a weasel, his fur slicked back from a swim in the water. And I fell out of the sky, feeling terrible and lonely and proud all at the same time. And when I was finished, I went to a stream of cool water to wash my hands. And that was when I saw on the surface of the water that my eyes had become large and cold and golden and feathers grew from my face, sweeping up from around my eyes like the petals of pale-mouthed flowers. I struck at the reflection with my hands and saw how the water dripped, glistening from the tips, washing away the blood.

I can't remember much else of what I dreamt that night but when I got up the next morning, the coldness and the loneliness stayed inside of me. And I knew what I would have to do; it's really what I knew all along: I would have to go after Pachinko—to stay close and wait and watch no matter how long it took until he led me to the charm. I knew, though, from what Mr. Jeh said that the Pachinko wouldn't be up before one in the afternoon so I had plenty of time to sit and be nervous. At first I wished Barney was there and then I realized it was just as well because he might lose his temper and do something he'd be sorry for. I was just getting ready to go when a very sleepy-looking Booger knocked at my door around noon to invite me to breakfast. I suppose her mom felt obligated to feed me once so I thought that I might as well get it over with.

Breakfast went okay. Booger's mom wasn't a bad person—just a little crazy about washing and dusting. And she really seemed worried about Paw-Paw, whom she called Auntie—not that we were related but it was just a name you used for an older woman in English.

"You know I've got a vacancy on the second floor. One with a bathroom. Only cost you five dollars more."

I didn't tell her that we were already paying out ten dollars more than we could really afford for the place we had now. I suppose she was already cutting down the price just to let us have the new apartment. "We like our place best. You know how hard it is for an old person to change."

"Don't I know it," Mrs. Chew sighed. "You should see my husband's mother. It's easier arguing with a stone." She poured more milk into my glass. "But how are you doing? Hospitals are so expensive nowadays."

When I first came into Chinatown, I used to get mad at people being so nosy. But many of the people in Chinatown easily accepted that kind of inquisitiveness between close friends and kin—and an older person could assume that they were close whether you wanted it or not. Since then I'd learned how to slide around those questions like any other Chinese. "What's the good of having rich sons and daughters if they can't give you a little money."

I glanced at the clock and saw it was already one in the afternoon so it was time to be out looking for Jack's Pool Hall. I felt a little owlish something inside me begin to stir. I finished my milk and got up. "I really can't thank you enough."

"You only had one piece of cake," Mrs. Chew accused me.

"One more ounce and I'd burst."

"Where are you going?" Booger asked.

"Oh, to the library."

"Good," Booger said before I could stop her, "I'll go with you. I can return some of my books." And there was nothing I could do but smile politely while Mrs. Chew was there, but inside I felt like screaming.

I was tempted when I came back down from our apartment not to stop by for Booger but that would have been too rude, so I rang their doorbell and found to my surprise that Booger wasn't ready yet. Mrs. Chew told me she was brushing out her hair! And then when Booger came out of the bathroom, she had to find her books. And then she had to model and explain the fashionableness of her new coat. It was about a half hour later before we finally got out the front door.

When we reached the mouth of the alley, I stopped, waiting for Booger with her pile of books to catch up. I took the top book for a moment. It was on costumes through the ages. The second was on posture. The next was a book on skin care. The last was on modeling.

"Just curious," Booger said, embarrassed.

I dumped the book on top of the pile in her arms. "I'm not really going to the library."

"Where are you going then?"

"To Jack's Pool Hall. Do you know where it is?"

Booger looked craftily. "Yes."

"Well, where is it?"

"Only if I can go with you, Casey."

"What would you want to do down there?"

She shrugged with difficulty because of the books. "You've seen and done so much and me, I just read about that stuff."

"This isn't some Saturday-morning cartoon. It could be dangerous. I'm staking the place out."

She really licked that up. "Great." She started up the steep hill. "But before I show you where Jack's is, I gotta return these books. They're due today."

"I ought to be down there right now."

She went on trudging up the hill. "You can take a half hour coming with me or you can spend the rest of the day asking people where Jack's is."

I didn't have much choice except to run after Booger and walk up with her to the library.

The library was this funny little brown brick building. The street level was closed off, and used for cutting up corpses for all I knew. Stairs curved up on either side from the street to a second-floor balcony where the library doors actually were. I stood on the balcony, my stomach against the stone railing, looking out at the cable cars clacking by, straining under hordes of shivering, sport-shirted or frocked tourists. They always come out to San Francisco expecting it to be as warm as L.A.

Booger came out a while later with a big, fat blue book under her arm that looked about four inches thick. I made her hold up the spine so I could read the title. "What do you want with a book on Florida birds?"

"It was the biggest book that I could swing. I figured I might need a weapon."

"Which way?" was all I said.

"To Grant first."

I started down the steps and she followed me. "Casey, you're not mad at me, are you?"

"No, no." I hurried across the street over the cable-car tracks. I could hear the cables rattling in their channels underneath the street. "What makes you think that?"

Booger was puffing beside me, holding on to her book with both arms. "Take it easy then, will you? This book is heavy."

Feeling guilty, I stopped, waiting impatiently for her to catch up. She meant well, I guess. We walked down the hill for a little while past the fruit stand where the horde of little old men and women squeezed the fruit faster than the owner could stop them. Booger glanced at me.

"There *is* something wrong," she said. "I can feel it."

"There's nothing wrong." I started across Stockton.

"No, no, really, what is it?" She pestered me with questions all the while we crossed the street. Finally when we reached the other curb, I couldn't take it anymore.

"All right, if you have to know. Why do you . . . why do you always have to act like a Booger Chew all the time?"

She stood there forlornly, her big book clutched in her arms. "I couldn't help being named that."

"Yeah, yeah, I know." I felt about two feet lower after saying that. "Look, I didn't think. I'm sorry."

"I mean your parents called you Casey. That's an adventurous name."

"It's not so great." I started on down the hill for Grant. I looked at her over my shoulder. "You coming along or not?"

She kept on talking while we walked—she always talked whenever she got nervous. "I mean, my great-aunt named me. I wish my parents had more guts to say no to her. Who wants to be called Tallulah Bankhead? And then I got stuck with that other, utterly horrid name."

It was funny but while Booger kept on talking, I began to feel sorry for her. My life wasn't in the greatest shape and yet I felt more in tune with things than she did. "Look," I said, "you really want to know how I got my American name? My dad named me after Casey Stengel 'cause while he was managing the Yankees, Dad won a lot of bets—they helped pay off the hospital bills when I was born." I added, "I've never told that to anyone." It was also why I preferred my Chinese name, only I didn't think Booger needed to know that.

I glanced at Booger to see if she was laughing, but she wasn't. She looked thoughtful. "At least they named me after a woman," she said. It seemed to cheer her up and I felt like I had made up for before.

"Yeah, and you ever see a picture of Casey Stengel? He looks like an old beat-up baseball glove. At least you've got somebody who's glamorous."

"I guess things could be worse," she agreed.

Though it was already the early afternoon, it seemed like people were just getting up, but then most everyone in Chinatown seemed to stay up all night, working in a restaurant, or playing games of Mah-Jong or singing or talking. Right now was the drowsy time when the shops unlocked their doors one by one and slid back their folding iron fences—opening to the sunlight like barnacles opening up to the first wash of the sea.

We stopped on Grant for a funny old yellow traffic light with the red and green lights set beside one another like eyes. It never did much good controlling traffic. Almost all the time I'd see this little old, hundred-pound man or woman launch themselves off the curb as fearless as some giant hawk expecting all the cars and trucks to huddle like frightened rabbits.

The high morning fog was finally burning away and the sunshine was beginning to come down. I stuffed my hands into my jeans and turned my face up toward the strip of blue sky. Booger unbuttoned the top button of her coat.

"You ever think about changing your name."

"I don't know," Booger said.

"I remember reading somewhere that all the big-name models have just one name. Maybe you ought to pick out one."

"I'm never really going to be a model." Booger shook her head.

"Well, maybe if you changed your name, you'd change your luck. Ever think of that?"

"Sometimes," she finally admitted.

"Ten to one you picked out a name for yourself."

Booger smiled shyly. "Well, yeah."

"Why don't you let me call you that name in private. Get into practice having someone use it on you." I nudged her with my elbow. "Come on. I won't tell anyone. I can't because you know the secret about how I really got my American name."

"You promise under pain of death not to tell?" she asked me.

"Wild horses couldn't drag it out of me."

"I'd be satisfied if no one in our class did that." When I nodded my head, she swallowed and leaned forward and whispered, "I always liked Talia." She said it like *Ta-lee-ah.* "That sounds so exotic, you know."

It was exactly the kind of name a Booger Chew would want to use. Still if she wanted me to use that name for her, I would. "It sure is exotic," I agreed.

The light finally changed and we crossed the street so we were right by the Italian Market, which, as far as I knew, never had an Italian inside of it. It was run by Chinese for Chinese and you could see the plucked ducks hanging from hooks on the walls like pale-pink footballs. Air had been pumped in between the skin and the actual body so that when the ducks were finally cooked, the skin would be especially crisp and part easily from the meat.

Below Grant, it was mostly apartment buildings of about three or four stories. A couple of them had storefronts with curtains filling them and from inside came the hum of sewing machines so I knew they were shops like Paw-Paw worked in. We stopped in the middle of the block and Booger nodded at a building across the street that had a basement with iron doors that swung up and out, revealing a set of stone steps leading down even further. "That's Jack's."

"We can't stand out here all the time." I looked around and saw a little alley just behind us. "Let's wait in there."

"In there?" Booger glanced at her new coat.

"You can't be fashionable in this business."

"I suppose," Booger said doubtfully, following me in.

Of course, Mr. Jeh was already there. He stood with his hands clasped behind his back, studying the brick wall before him and trying his best to look at ease among the garbage cans.

"Good afternoon, Mr. Jeh," I said.

"What are you doing here?" He frowned. "Maybe you get into trouble down here."

"That's why I brought along a bodyguard. This is my friend Tallulah Chew."

Mr. Jeh nodded to her and then rubbed his chin. "Tallulah. You Mamie's little granddaughter?"

"Yes, you knew Grandmom?"

"Oh, yes. Good singer." He explained to me, "Bunch of us used get together and listen records of Chinese opera. Sometimes she sing."

Talia finally put two and two together. "Are we waiting for your grandnephew to show up?"

"Yes," Mr. Jeh said in a way that even shut up Talia.

We moved further back in the alley, inside a dark doorway against a large, corrugated iron door with NO PARKING painted over its front in big, broad strokes.

"What goes on in Jack's anyway?" I asked.

Mr. Jeh pushed his lips out thoughtfully for a moment. "They shoot pool. Play pinball. Smoke cigarettes. Think of how to get in more trouble, you bet. No one ever goes in before three. All no-goods asleep." Mr. Jeh settled down into a squat, his back against the door. I tried it but my legs ached where they joined my hips so I just stood up with my back against the doorway for support. Poor Talia, though, couldn't even do that because of her new coat. She had to stand up straight. She opened her book and held it awkwardly in both hands, sighing. "I hope there's something interesting to read in here."

It was about an hour later before the first couple of boys sauntered down the stairs, both of them in the tight black jeans and black Windbreakers those kinds of kids wore. Their hair was slicked up with grease so that it was like some oily shag rug. One of them led a bulldog that waddled along. It wasn't till another hour later that a big purple Cadillac came tooling up the street. Outside of Jack's was a white sign on a stand saying "NO PARKING by Order of the SFPD." The Pachinko got out of the car, opened the trunk, put the sign into it, and then parked the car.

"His space reserved," Mr. Jeh explained as he stood up.

When the Pachinko went down the steps, I felt myself tensing, like an owl hovering waiting to strike, but nothing happened for a whole hour.

"Stakeouts are usually more interesting on TV," Talia said, finishing the third boring chapter. "Things happen a lot faster."

"I wait forever and ever. You bet." Mr. Jeh nodded his head once to seal that proclamation.

"Maybe I ought to just go in and see what's happening," I said. I was beginning to feel jittery.

"You ruin everything," Mr. Jeh said sternly. I settled back against the door and crossed my arms, trying to prepare myself for a long wait.

Finally the Pachinko came out of Jack's, doing his James Dean imitation again. He didn't walk out like regular people but came out in a slouching swagger, like he was about to go on camera any moment. He went to the phone booth on the corner, took out something from his jacket pocket and jiggled it around in the telephone, and then dialed a number. He straightened suddenly in the booth as if he were excited and when he stepped out of the booth, he was walking along fast with some definite purpose in mind. It was the most deliberate kind of thing I'd ever seen the Pachinko do.

"Let's go," Mr. Jeh said. I pushed myself off the door, feeling as if I were about to take wing.

"Wait for me." Talia slammed her book shut.

Mr. Jeh held out his hand. "You better let me carry it."

"No, no, I'm really all right."

"Give it to him," I said. "He can carry it and still walk fast."

Reluctantly Talia held the book up with both hands. Mr. Jeh took it and tucked it underneath his arm.

We set off after the Pachinko, hurrying to get closer to him before he got to Grant, where we might lose him in the swirling mobs. As it was, we almost lost him at the light. He ran across the crosswalk on a yellow light and by the time we got to the corner, the cars were already starting across the intersection.

"We can't let him get more than half a block ahead," I said to Mr. Jeh.

Mr. Jeh said nothing but squeezed his way between two fat indignant ladies and stepped into the crosswalk.

"He'll get run over," Talia said. I grabbed her arm and pulled her after me off the curb.

A fat bronze-colored Mercedes-Benz started accelerating toward the intersection just as Mr. Jeh walked into the middle of the crosswalk. The driver, a fat, pompous-looking businessman, hit the brakes, coming to a screeching halt, but you almost couldn't hear that because one fat hand kept pounding his horn. A powered window rolled down and he stuck his head out. "Hey, what's the matter, grandpa? Don't you know you don't walk on a red light?"

Mr. Jeh stopped, hawked, and very calmly spat on the window. The businessman's jaw dropped. The cars behind him began to honk.

"Come on, Mr. Jeh." We caught up with him in the crosswalk and Talia and I dragged him the rest of the way to the other curb. Behind us the businessman tried to start his car again but it had stalled. I could hear the engine grinding as he tried to start it again while even more cars began honking.

Mr. Jeh shook us off. "What you think I am, old or something? I not need help to walk."

I looked for the Pachinko. He was turning into an alley. "We'd better hurry."

"Ha, you see which of us get out of breath." Mr. Jeh leaned forward and started off like an Olympic walker up the steep hill. By the time we got to the alley, Talia and I were both panting but Mr. Jeh was breathing as easily as if we were just strolling. It was almost as if he drew his energy from the air like Paw-Paw said. The alley ran for two blocks, crossing a street in its middle. The Pachinko turned up another steep street when he came out of the alley and then ducked into another side alley.

"Wait," Mr. Jeh said when we reached its mouth. We peeped around the corner and saw the Pachinko impatiently jabbing his finger at the doorbell of an apartment house. Someone spoke over the intercom near the doorbell and the Pachinko leaned forward and spoke into the mouthpiece. Eventually there was a buzz and the Pachinko opened the door with a quick jerk and went in. I ran across the alley, taking the narrow sidewalk in one jump. Lucky for us the door swung shut slowly so I could stop it just before it locked. I held it while Talia and Mr. Jeh hurried up.

"All right. Now." Mr. Jeh jerked his head toward the building. I pushed the door open and we stepped into a small lobby that smelled faintly of urine. The paint on the walls was cracking and in some places the plaster had fallen away, revealing the wooden slats. I tiptoed forward and looked up the light well of the stairs that wound up and up. I could just see the back of the Pachinko's head two flights up. I started up quietly and Mr. Jeh and Talia followed me, all of us with our faces turned up intently on the Pachinko.

We stopped on the stairs below the third landing, looking up through the banisters at the Pachinko, who was talking earnestly with a hefty, middle-aged man. The man had greased his thinning hair back from his forehead, trying to cover his bald spot. A pair of red suspenders kept his floppy pants up. The man grunted and shook his head, sticking his cigar back in his mouth.

The Pachinko leaned forward, arguing with the man in low whispers. The man's cigar twitched angrily. He wagged a warning finger at the Pachinko. The Pachinko slapped his hand away and sneered something at the man. The man shook his fist at the Pachinko and growled something but the Pachinko only laughed. And then the man shoved the Pachinko. The Pachinko would have started back at the man, but the man put his hand inside his coat. The Pachinko froze in a crouch, ready to jump on the man.

That was when Mr. Jeh started up the steps with the book still tucked under one arm, the other arm behind his back. And for the first time that I had ever seen, he stomped along like an old man. The fat man glanced over the railing down at Mr. Jeh. The Pachinko tensed but the man turned back to the Pachinko, who stood still again. The Pachinko did not turn around—I guess he didn't dare. Impatiently, the fat man stepped into his doorway, his back against the door to give the old man room to pass. The Pachinko straightened up suddenly, startled to see his great-uncle there. The fat man twisted his head slightly to

get a better look at the old man and saw he wasn't a regular ten-
ant of the building. But Mr. Jeh pounced then. He struck out
with the big heavy Florida-bird book, clipping the fat man on the
side of the head. The fat man crumpled up. Mr. Jeh leaned over
the railing. "You have clean handkerchief?" he called down to us.

"I've got some Kleenex." Talia fished around in her left coat
pocket and pulled out a tissue, waving it over her head.

"Good." Mr. Jeh waved his hand. "Bring it up to me."

The Pachinko looked disgusted when we joined him on the
landing. "What is this? A reunion?"

Mr. Jeh took the Kleenex from Talia and wiped fastidiously at
the cover of the book. "You see how greasy that man's head
was?"

The Pachinko bent over the fat man and felt around in his
coat pocket. He took out a small gun.

"I take that." Mr. Jeh held out one hand.

"Now, Uncle. I appreciate your helping—" the Pachinko
mumbled.

"I save you, boy." Mr. Jeh hefted the book in one hand. "You
not as tough as you think." They stared at one another.

The Pachinko finally dropped the whole James Dean routine
and stood up straight and spoke clearly again. "All right. All
right." He smoothed back his hair nervously and passed the gun
on to his great-uncle, who pocketed it. He handed the book
back to Talia. "Thank you."

Talia lifted her eyebrows toward me. "You see. I told you we'd
need the book."

Mr. Jeh clasped his hands behind his back. "Now you tell me
what go on here, boy."

The Pachinko jerked his head at Talia and me. "First get rid
of the kids."

"They stay. You tell her everything too."

"Look, Gramps—"

Mr. Jeh slapped his grandnephew's arm. "Are you going to
tell me, you no-good, or not?"

"Uncle, it's not like you think. I mean this guy knows where
the owl charm is. He's been checking out possible buyers so
just trust me on this. Get rid of the kids."

"Why should I trust you anymore? You told me you not know
anything about it."

"I didn't. Not then. I just had suspicions so I had a couple of
friends keep their eyes and ears open for me and I just checked
with them every now and then."

"Well, why you not come and tell us?"

The apartment door opened and Barney stepped out and knelt on one leg by his friend, feeling the egg growing there on the side of his head. "Did you have to hit him so hard?"

I stared at Barney but Barney wouldn't look up at me. I poked him in the shoulder. "Barney, what are you doing here? Your last postcard came from way down south."

"Got a lift from this trucker I knew." Barney helped his friend to sit up groggily. "Ever since my last phone call, I kept worrying about how you were getting along in Chinatown. Finally, I just couldn't take it any longer so I came up to check for myself." Barney slipped his friend's arm over his shoulders and, holding the door open with his foot, he helped his friend back into the room. There was just an old beat-up chest of drawers and an old, heavy iron bedstead in the room. On the floor was a blanket, where I guess Barney slept.

I followed Barney into the room as he and his friend shuffled across the cracked linoleum floor. "Barney, if you were really so worried, you could have called again—collect even."

The bed creaked as Barney dropped his friend onto it. "I'd already dumped you on your Paw-Paw. How's it look if I started sticking her with big long-distance calls too?"

I knew how pig-headedly proud Barney could be sometimes about these things. "Damn it, Barney. I wish you'd at least stayed in one place long enough to get one of my letters then. That way you could have found out I kinda got used to Chinatown."

"You did?" Barney sounded surprised.

"Yeah. Kinda," I said.

"Well, I wish I couldn've gotten one of those letters then. It'd have taken a big load off my mind." Barney sighed. "But you know how that goes, baby. I had to keep ahead of the bills." Barney lifted his friend's legs on top of the bed and straightened them out. "Couldn't stay long in one place." He looked around the room for something else to do so he wouldn't have to think when he talked to me. Only there wasn't anything else.

"Why didn't you call me when you first got here?" I demanded. I was beginning to get mad at him.

"I was, baby. Honestly. But I wanted a little dough first so I could make up to you for having to stay behind in Chinatown. I tried to borrow some dough but it was no go." He lifted his shoulders up and down once. "Then it all just kinda happened."

I got this real creepy feeling then: like my spine had grown all kinds of little legs and they were wriggling and crawling, trying to rip my spine loose from my back. "Happened? What do you mean?"

Barney rubbed the stubble on his chin with his thumb. "Like I said. I just wanted a little pocket money for you and me. Maybe get a hamburger and talk together, that's how it started, I swear. So I went to look in your Paw-Paw's change drawer—just to borrow till my luck got going again—and then I found the charm. It was just what we all needed."

"No." I shook my head real hard. "No. You're just covering up for your friend. You wouldn't have done that to Paw-Paw. Not for anything."

"I did it, I tell you." Barney grabbed my arms and gave me a little shake when I tried to drop my eyes. "Look at me, baby. I'm the one who did it, but I didn't mean to." Barney bent his knees a little so he could look into my eyes. "I got this hot streak coming on. I just know it. I got into this game in L.A., see. Just twenty dollars in my pocket and in one hour I wound up three hundred ahead. But then my luck kinda stalled."

His luck stalled. I'd heard that excuse umpteen million times. I turned my face away from him to stare stubbornly at a crack in the wall. I didn't want to look at him. I didn't want to hear him. I didn't even want to think. But somehow I found myself asking "How much do you owe, Barney?"

"Another grand, baby." Barney dropped his hands away from my arms. He straightened up and then tried to step around to where I was looking so he could make me face him; but I twisted my head quickly in the other direction. I wished I hadn't. I was looking straight at the chest of drawers. On its top I saw an old pack of cigarettes, some small change, and a little flat object wrapped up in a familiar-looking scarf. "Baby, I could have paid off Big Mike and that other guy down south both." Barney was pleading now. "My friend here was going to help me sell it. It would have been okay. See, as soon as I got the money and got out of town, I'd have tipped off the cops and they would have gotten the charm back for you because it was stolen."

I could feel the stinging at the corners of my eyes, like someone was digging around with needles. "You couldn't be the thief. You didn't have to steal." I turned to face Barney. "I mean you could have just borrowed the small change you needed from that friend of yours, the one that is loaning me five bucks every week."

Barney stuck his hands in his pockets and wrinkled his forehead as if he were puzzled. "I don't know what you're talking about, baby. If I knew somebody who'd have done that, I'd have asked them. But I don't. All my friend here would do was let me sleep on his floor; and then he offered to help fence the charm if I'd give him a cut."

I couldn't figure that out so I left it alone.

The others had crowded into the doorway, staying a few feet away from me and Barney. I wheeled on the Pachinko. "You knew it was Barney, didn't you?"

"I had my suspicions, Casey." He shrugged his shoulders guiltily. "I'd seen him around town the day before your Paw-Paw got hurt; and when you didn't seem to know he was here, I figured there was something wrong. But I thought maybe I could get back the charm without having to tell you."

"You can't keep people from learning things like that," I complained angrily.

"You're right, Casey," the Pachinko said. "I'm sorry."

I told myself it wasn't fair to take my anger out on the Pachinko. It was just that there were these tears in my eyes and it made me even madder to think anyone would see them. So I just stood for a while, shutting my eyes real tight and tilting up my head, hoping that the tears would drain away.

I don't know what I had figured on doing when I caught up with the thief. Maybe I had hoped to be like the princess of the streets in that movie and kick in his head. Or at least get the satisfaction of turning him over to the cops. But now . . . I'd caught my prey, and it was a truly fitting one for a child of the owl, because it was my own father. Only it just *couldn't* be. I opened my eyes and swung them down to look at Barney. "I won't believe it was you, Barney. I mean, the thief put Paw-Paw in the hospital and you wouldn't have done that. Not to Paw-Paw. She used to defend you all the time."

"I keep telling you, baby, I didn't plan any of it. It just sorta happened." Barney studied the pattern on the floor linoleum for a while. "I wish I could tell you that you were right. But it was me, baby. I didn't mean to push her that hard. And you don't know how bad it made me feel when I heard she wound up in the hospital."

I felt real funny when he said that. The closest thing to it was when Barney and me had once stayed in this old boarding house with floorboards so rotten that with each step I thought the floor would fall apart in dust and splinters. But this was a lot worse because it was like everything, just everything, had crumbled. "Oh, Barney." I found my hands balling themselves into fists. "Barney, why couldn't it have been your friend? That would have left me something." I caught Talia looking at me. I turned away quickly. The tears were starting to slip over the corners of my eyes and I didn't want any of them to see.

Even now, though, Barney couldn't see anything really wrong in what he had done. "Don't worry, baby," Barney started going on. "My luck is changing." He held up one hand and put his thumb and forefinger close together. "I know I'm just this much away from striking it big, and then we'll live in that penthouse—"

I could hear myself shouting. "Barney, don't you see? It never mattered to me about living in the penthouse. The only important thing was being together. You and me."

"I'll make it up to you, baby. Just you wait," Barney insisted. But I'd heard that all before.

I struck out then, letting my words act like talons to slash at Barney. "That's a lie, Barney. All your life you've been telling yourself lies. And you've been telling me lies."

I ran out of the room then, taking the steps two at a time.

Chapter Seven

I

I hurt inside.

I hurt inside and at first I didn't know why.

It felt just like there was a real owl inside me trying to bite and claw its way out and while it was tearing its way through my chest, I couldn't get my head to working. And while all that was going on, part of me knew I was walking through Chinatown and made me stop at traffic lights and steered me clear of bumping into anyone, but it was like most of me was far, far away. It wasn't so much like I was wandering through Chinatown; it was more like I was floating through a world of ghosts and dream people.

But finally I settled down in about the only green spot in Chinatown, which was the square. Though there were plenty of old people around, Paw-Paw's club wasn't there because they were either up at the hospital or doing something else. I hugged my knees against my chest and just sat there for a long time, and eventually some thoughts finally drifted clear where I could get hold of them. What got to me was that Barney had been doing all that stuff for me. I mean, it was like I had caused Paw-Paw to go into the hospital just because I lived and breathed.

And I found myself wishing more and more that I could just leave all this behind me. I wished I really was an owl so that an Owl Spirit would come to me. I knew just how the Owl Spirit ought to look too—like Jeanie when she was young, only the Owl Spirit would have larger eyes and her mouth might push out just a little more in a beakish way. And she'd be holding up a feather dress and I'd put it on and fly away from here and never come back. Only no matter how hard I tried to hold on to that dream, it wouldn't stay. It kept fading away.

"Casey!" I heard Talia call. I started to get up but Talia was already skipping across the lawn. "We've been looking all over for you."

I started to rub at the grass stains on my jeans in an annoyed way. "I wonder how I'm going to get those spots out."

Talia tugged at my arm. "Casey, will you listen to me?"

"I don't want to talk to anyone but Paw-Paw."

"That's what we've been trying to set up, dummy."

"You can fix it up for me?"

"My cousin is an intern up there." Talia turned her head and called up the street. "Angela. She's here."

And this tall woman pushed her way through the crowds on the sidewalk around the square and walked with an efficient air onto the lawn. She had on a long convoy coat and she had her hands stuffed into the deep pockets. She smiled pleasantly at me as she stepped across the grass. "Hello, Casey. I've heard a lot about you."

"You don't hold it against me?"

"Your being a good friend of hers? I don't see why I should."

"She said you could help me see Paw-Paw."

She scratched the tip of her nose. "I can't quite do that. Rules are rules."

"I'll cut off all my hair and take a bath in rubbing alcohol if that'll kill all the germs."

"You don't have to do anything that drastic." Angela had a nice smile. "I'll see she's wheeled near a phone for a while and then you can talk to her that way."

It was time to stop feeling sorry for myself and take what I could get. "That's really great of you to go to all this trouble," I said, trying to keep the disappointment out of my voice.

I didn't want to call from our place because our phone was a party line so anyone could overhear us. I could have called from Talia's place but that would have meant explaining things to her mom and worse yet—having her listen while I talked to Paw-Paw. I didn't want that. The story would be all over Chinatown soon enough—if it wasn't already. So I wound up calling from the telephone booth across the street from the hospital.

It was late afternoon so the red-colored, Chinese-looking lamps on either side of the steps had already gone on. There was a red-tiled roof above the entrance, kind of like the Chinese gates you see in books and movies, and the walls themselves were painted cream or yellow—no white because white was the traditional color of mourning among the Chinese and the older people thought it was bad luck to have it around. But otherwise Chinese Hospital could have been a good, small hospital anywhere in the city.

Talia stood beside me and glanced down at her wristwatch. "Okay, it's four-thirty. Angie should have everything set up now."

I pulled back the folding door of the booth and put my hand inside my pocket. But all I had was a fifty-cent piece and some pennies. "Has anyone got change?" I asked. But Talia and Mr. Jeh and the Pachinko didn't have any change either.

"Wait," said the Pachinko. He slipped a hairpin out of Talia's hair before she could stop him. "This is one of those old telephones so I can pull a certain trick." He wiggled one of the balled ends of the hairpin until it broke off. Then he bent over the old black telephone and stuck it into the lock of the coin box, jiggling the hairpin around till he got a dial tone. "There." He stood back triumphantly.

"It would have been faster if I'd just gone to get some change," I said. But I dialed the number that Angela had written on a slip of paper. Eventually I got through the switchboard to the phone. I heard Angela at the other end.

"Hello, Casey. Here's your grandmother."

I closed the telephone-booth door and the Pachinko and Talia and Mr. Jeh tactfully withdrew to study the plastic ships and tanks set up in a laundry window. I suppose the kids of the owner made them. I leaned back against the glass side. "Paw-Paw?"

"Girl, is that you?" Her voice came over deeper on the phone than it usually was and there was a little static that seemed to drip from her voice. It was hard to think of a disembodied voice as Paw-Paw.

"Why haven't you been up?" she asked.

I sighed. "They won't let me. I have to be a certain age before they'll let me up."

Paw-Paw left the phone for a moment and I could hear her quiet, urgent voice in the background. I suppose she was talking to Angela, but finally Paw-Paw came back on. She sounded resigned to the fact that they couldn't break the rules for her. "They say I can leave pretty soon."

"That's great, Paw-Paw. Just great."

Paw-Paw sighed at the other end. "There's so much to say to one another I don't know where to start."

I turned my back away from the others so they couldn't even see my lips moving. "I saw Barney, Paw-Paw."

"Oh?" Paw-Paw said carefully.

"You knew it was Barney, didn't you? That's why you didn't want us to call the police."

"I thought it was him. But I wanted to be sure before I said anything."

"You're not mad at him?"

Paw-Paw took a long time to answer and her voice somehow sounded gentle even over the phone. "Yes, I was mad at first, but if there's one thing I've learned over the years it's that you can't afford to stay mad at anyone. Barney can't help himself, girl. Gambling's like a sickness with him. You or I could leave a game of cards anytime, but Barney couldn't—no more than a starving dog can leave a bone. I knew that a long time ago. So did your mommy." Paw-Paw waited a moment. "Do you understand?"

"I don't know. He hurt you."

"He got scared. He didn't mean to hurt me, but he forgot I was an old woman with bones that are like glass." Paw-Paw paused. "And remember this, Child of the Owl, an owl is hurt by others as much as the owl hurts."

I studied the floor of the telephone booth where somebody's gum had turned into a black bump. I rubbed it with the sole of my sneaker and just held on to the phone receiver, feeling like Paw-Paw's own quiet strength flowed over the telephone lines and through the receiver into me. Finally, I looked back up at the telephone and the numbers etched by a knife across its old black surface. "Paw-Paw, it looks like you'll be stuck with me for a long time."

"Do you mind living in Chinatown?" Paw-Paw asked.

I drew a figure in the dust on the window. Outside I could see Talia and the Pachinko and Mr. Jeh standing around, talking to one another. Remembering how they all tried to help me, I knew I wasn't alone. And for a moment I felt what Mr. Jeh had said that first time I had met him in the square: I could feel the earth in Chinatown holding me up and it was like up to now, I'd only been placed above it without taking or giving any support. Chinatown was the first place I'd ever had roots in because Barney and I had always been too busy before this to stay put. And roots could be a pesky thing holding you down, or they could feed you and let you grow strong until it came time to leave. I turned to face the hospital again. "I'm getting to like it here."

"That's good. Are you eating all right?"

"Yes, Paw-Paw." I nodded my head as if she could see me and I assured her about the other things that worried her: like if I was dressing warm—yes, I was—and whether I left the gas oven on at night when I went to bed—no, I didn't. And maybe at some other time all those pesky questions would have gotten to me but right then those questions were just what I needed—like Paw-Paw was spinning a lightweight, yet strong, silk cocoon about me to keep me warm and safe.

I guess it was so long since I had let myself cry that I found myself crying again. Twice in the same day—it was humiliating. I wiped at my eyes with the back of my sleeve but the more I tried to stop, the more tears I could feel coming out.

It was funny but Paw-Paw seemed to understand even though she couldn't see me. "Don't be afraid to cry, girl," she said over the phone. And now it was like she wasn't in the hospital anymore, but somewhere deep inside me. "Never be afraid to cry. Just don't let that be an excuse not to do anything."

Suddenly I could feel the warm come bubbling up from inside. Funny, but I don't remember ever telling anyone before—not even Barney. "Paw-Paw, I love you."

"I love you too, girl. Now you be careful."

Neither of us wanted to be the first to hang up, but finally Paw-Paw said, "You hang up first, Casey."

"All right." I hung up the phone and wiped at my eyes again but I was pretty dry now though my darn nose had gotten stuffy. It was time to pull back on the folding door and go outside, but for a moment I studied my friends—I guess they had earned the right to be called friends after what they had gone through for me. The fierce, proud old pagan, Mr. Jeh, and Talia in the newest, fanciest coat and the Pachinko, his hair arched up like the bristling back of a cat. Then I stepped outside and they turned to me.

"How is she?" Mr. Jeh asked, but since he got to see her, he already knew she was all right. The person he was really asking about was me.

"She's okay and so am I."

"You know what you need?" the Pachinko said. "You need a super float over at Fong and Fong's. All of you."

"Not that place," grumbled Mr. Jeh. "They want ten cents for a cup of coffee now and no refills. I don't like clip joints."

"Don't you worry, Uncle. One of my buddies is the soda jerk there. He'll see we're all treated right." He reached a hand into his jacket pocket. "I almost forgot. I had the clasp fixed." He took out the owl charm wrapped in Paw-Paw's red scarf. When I freed it, the tiger smile seemed to stir for a moment in the late afternoon sun as if it had been cold and had missed a person's warmth.

II

PAW-PAW'S hospital bill was a whopper and since Paw-Paw's money was already stretched pretty thin and since we weren't sure when she'd be able to go back to the sewing-machine shop, we asked Phil about helping us when he came to visit Paw-Paw.

"Momma, you know I'd do anything for you, but some investments haven't been paying off and I took a beating on the stock market and now with Annette going to college and Pamela wanting to go to that fancy girls' school . . ." Phil squirmed on the chair. "I'll give what I can, but I don't think it can be much."

"Well, they have different installment plans." I shoved the sheet over to him with the figures. Paw-Paw didn't say anything—she hated business, readily turning it over to me. Phil chewed his lip as he studied the figures. "I couldn't do more than help you with the monthly installments." He put the sheet down and looked at us in what seemed genuine distress. "Momma, I'm really sorry—"

Paw-Paw took the sheet and stroked the back of his hand. "It's all right, boy. You take care of my grandchildren first."

It was more or less the same thing with Phil's sister and his brother down in L.A. Both of them had good excuses why they couldn't send much money.

I sat staring at the telephone for a long time after Paw-Paw had made her last phone call. "If we were in China," I said, "they'd have to help."

"But we're not in China." Paw-Paw placed the telephone firmly back in the wall alcove. "We're in America where everyone is supposed to have his own car and his own house and every fancy gadget that everyone else has." It was almost as if she pitied her children. "Don't judge them too harshly. In their heads, they all carry two pictures of what a family should be— an American and a Chinese one—and the two don't always match; and that probably makes them the most miserable of all."

Before that, I'd never seen the funny side to Phil the Pill, but now I did. He was short and round-faced like an owl and his big, thick horn-rimmed glasses made his eyes look big and owlish. And I remembered how he'd always be hopping around whenever he came up for his weekly visit to Paw-Paw. He'd be sitting there with his cigarette, chain-smoking and talking about the new rugs they were getting or asking her if she liked his new suit. Then suddenly he'd break off in the middle of a sentence to hop to the window to check on his Lincoln double-parked in the alley. The slightest noise—a kid shouting, a whir of pigeon wings—had him out of his seat and checking the paint job. It was like there was nothing he valued inside of himself; it was only the things outside—like he could make up for being empty inside by having a lot of stuff outside. And he fluttered and hooted like some nervous little owl who got mad every time one of *his* leaves fell off *his* tree.

Paw-Paw got up and shuffled over to the table. With a great deal of pleasure she lit up a cigarette, exhaling the smoke gratefully. She hadn't been able to smoke at all in the hospital so she was making up for lost time. The only thing that kept her from chain-smoking was the cost of the cigarettes. "And besides, things weren't so perfect in China." She left her cigarette in the ashtray and folded her hands on her lap as she leaned toward me. "How would you like to have a marriage arranged for you? That's the way it would have been in the old days in China." She picked up her cigarette again. "And anyway, the China you're talking about was gone a long time ago. It was changing even when I was a girl. The only place where the old China lives on is in the memories of the old people here and in the movies."

With my finger I slowly traced part of the design on the tablecloth. "Why do you have to be so understanding all the time, Paw-Paw?"

"I'm not. I get mad just like you, but like I told you, as I got older, I learned I couldn't just stay mad."

"I'm never going to forgive Phil and the others."

"Never is a long time." Paw-Paw lit up another cigarette from the stub of her old one.

"Since it wasn't Barney who sent the five dollars every week, it must've been one of your friends. Maybe that person would loan us the money."

Paw-Paw studied the cigarette smoke that eddied above her head as if she could read the answer there. "It must be Gilbert then."

"Gilbert!"

"He's not as bad as he likes to act." Paw-Paw knocked about half an inch of ash into the ashtray. "He's not one to take advantage of us for favors we owe him, but even so, you better tell him to stop. And we certainly can't ask him for the money for the hospital bill."

"It'll be better coming from you. Why me?"

"Why not you? You took the money."

"I guess," I said uncomfortably.

The buzzer began sounding insistently, but not in the regular pattern. I glanced at Paw-Paw. "Buzz the front door open and then put the chain on our door and only open it a crack." I did like she said, hearing heavy footsteps come up the stairs.

It was Barney. "Can I come in? I want to talk to you."

I was going to say no but Paw-Paw said from behind me, "Come in, Barney."

Reluctantly I slipped the chain back and opened the door. Barney came in and took off his cap, nodding apologetically to Paw-Paw. "How're you feeling?"

"All right, Barney. Would you like some tea?" she asked him.

"No, that's okay." He started to sit down on our bed.

"Over there." I pointed at the stool. He sat down on it while I closed the door. I took my place beside Paw-Paw.

"I'm sorry for what I've done." Barney twirled his cap nervously between his hands. "I didn't mean for any of this to happen."

"You're in trouble, aren't you?"

Barney flipped his cap onto the table. "I owe money, Paw-Paw."

"How much?"

"Two thousand."

Paw-Paw's eyebrows went up. "That much?"

"He doesn't know when to stop," I said.

"No, never did." Barney glanced up at me humbly. "I need you with me, baby. You always know when to make me stop."

"I'm not getting back together again with you, Barney—for the summer or forever."

"That's a long time, girl," Paw-Paw reminded me.

"I don't even want to see him," I told Paw-Paw, "not ever again."

"Casey!" Paw-Paw said sharply.

Barney pursed his lips and looked unhappily from me to Paw-Paw. "No, that's okay. I had it coming." He picked up his cap again, plucking at the lint on it. He didn't look at me while he talked. "What if I changed, baby? What if I gave up gambling?"

"You'll never change, Barney."

"I'd change for you, baby." Barney leaned his elbows on his knees, thrusting his head and body forward urgently. "You're all I got. I can take most anything as long as you're there . . . or even if I could just see you every now and then. I'll join that bunch, you know, Gamblers Anonymous. They help you kick the habit."

Barney's face looked too much like when he used to talk about the penthouse. I figured this was just another story he was making up for both of us to try and live in. "Even if you did manage to give up gambling, I still wouldn't see you. I can't trust you anymore. You really don't know when you do terrible things to people."

Barney pressed his lips together sullenly and drummed his fingers on the table. "I'm sorry for what I have to say, Paw-Paw," he said to her and then he looked up at me. "What use does your Paw-Paw have for that charm anyway? All she does is sit down at the square or sweat over a sewing machine. That charm belongs around the neck of some classy American broad, you know, someone young and pretty that wears all those fancy gowns and rides in limousines."

I was shocked by what Barney said and right in front of Paw-Paw too. "The owl charm is more than some stuff you can pick up in a ritzy store. The charm was given to us by the Owl Spirit."

"That's just superstition, baby," Barney insisted scornfully.

I could have reminded Barney about his own little plastic charm, but that didn't really get to the heart of the matter. "All right, suppose—just suppose—that the Owl Spirit wasn't an actual person." I glanced cautiously at Paw-Paw but her face had become an unreadable blank ever since Barney insulted her. "Even if she's not flesh and blood, she's still real. There's a little bit of her in me and in the Pachin—I mean, Gilbert. In you. Even in Paw-Paw. So I know there has to be an Owl Spirit, even if she's scattered in little bits and pieces in a lot of people. Only we don't usually have to face that fact until we hear her story. And the owl charm reminds us of that story. You can't buy that kind of lesson for a billion dollars."

"You trying to tell me that you think you're a real owl?" Barney scratched his forehead unhappily. "That's crazy."

I could see it wasn't any use to talk to Barney about what the owl charm meant to me and Paw-Paw. The story was like a mirror showing him his reflection: showing him that he was also a child of the owl. And he had turned his back on that image and tried to run away. He'd been running away all these years. And now when I tried to make him look at his real image again, he tried to say the mirror didn't exist; it was just superstition and those things were just make-believe—like ghosts. Well, sure, there are some silly superstitions, but just because a thing's old doesn't make it lose its meaning.

"You want to hear a crazy story, Barney? I'll tell you one. There's a whole bunch of people who like to pretend they're nothing but machines and that makes them feel so empty inside that they have to live in big houses, even penthouses, that they fill up with lots of junk, and the more junk they got, the bigger they feel. But what makes it sad is that they're not machines at all, but people, Barney, flesh-and-blood people."

"All right. Maybe Americans do like to have a lot of stuff. But so do the Chinese. Don't kid yourself, baby."

"Sure, and I know that. But some Chinese still know how to look deep inside themselves and I'm gonna be one of them." I put my hands on Paw-Paw's shoulders. "I'm a child of the owl."

Barney stared at me like he just couldn't figure me out—like I was now someone who only looked like his daughter. "But the owl story is just a story, baby," he insisted in his puzzled way.

"It's not a story, Barney," I tried to explain. "It tells me who I am. And that's worth more to me than penthouses and limousines."

Barney dropped his cap on the floor and he groped around for a moment before he managed to find it. "I think I better go." He shook his head, hurt and confused. And I knew suddenly what the Owl Spirit must have felt when she had left her "walker" home. But even so, she had gone through with it because it was the best thing. Barney mumbled his good-byes to us both and heaved himself up from the stool. When I closed the door, I looked at Paw-Paw. "I'm sorry for what he said."

"What he said was true." She lit herself another cigarette. "But I think what you said was truer. Still," she added, "no matter what he did, you should have been more respectful to your father."

I dropped down on our bed and picked up an old *Life* magazine from a pile that Phil had brought over—Paw-Paw could look at the pictures at least. "I'm sorry, Paw-Paw, but I'm not Shirley Temple."

"Who?"

"She's this kid with real curly hair and dimples who's always being sweet and kind and always forgiving people." I pretended to read through the magazine, flipping the pages over even though I wasn't looking at the pictures or the words.

Paw-Paw picked up the charm that lay on the table. As the charm slid off the tabletop, it made a metallic, hissing sound.

"I had hopes this would be yours one day, girl."

"I don't care if I get it, Paw-Paw. Just so long as someone in the family has it. Even Pamela. Don't sell it. Don't listen to Barney."

She weighed the charm in her hand and then put it down. "If I could get the right price for the charm, I might be able to help Barney."

"He'd gamble it away, Paw-Paw, trying to double it."

"I'm sure you know somebody reliable who could find those men Barney owes and pay them off."

"I guess, but . . . but"—I shrugged—"why bother?"

"Because no one should ever have to be all by themselves."
Paw-Paw spoke gently but firmly. "And maybe because a mother
shouldn't have to go around like a beggar to her children.
Maybe I can also have enough to pay off my bills too, you see?"

She was a small woman but I felt like it would have taken a
dozen bulldozers to try and move her aside: her roots seemed to
reach down all the way to the very bones of the earth. She knew
who she was and what she had to do—even if I didn't like it
much. Barney was dead wrong. If anyone had *class*, it was Paw-
Paw. I got up from the bed and gave her a hug. "Paw-Paw, I
hope I'm going to be like you when I finish growing up."

She stroked my hair back from my forehead and looked at me
unhappily and yet with affection. "I'm afraid you already are like
me. And that's a pity."

III

THE whole museum was air-conditioned and yet there still
was a dusty smell inside the museum director's office. A smell
of old dust mixing with furniture polish. Like the dusty air crept
in from the things in the museum past the filters of the air con-
ditioners. The huge, heavy curtains had been drawn back to re-
veal a funny kind of sky, because the clouds looked like wool
that had been combed and combined again into the finest white
threads and they just hung there in the blue sky.

The director sat behind a huge mahogany desk that made
him look more like a kid. He was really only Paw-Paw's height.
He was friendly and polite but a bit doubtful that it was worth
his talking to us. He sat back in his chair, his elbows on the
desk edge, pressing his fingertips together. "You understand
that we are already quite well stocked up on Ching artifacts."

Sherman, who was there without a fee to help us negotiate,
flicked some ash into a large bronze ashtray. "I'm not sure when
it was made," he said. "In all my years of dealing, I haven't seen
anything like it."

The director smiled. "Well, the fact alone that it's jade makes
it worth my while to look at it. And you've provided us with
some excellent pieces in the past." He looked expectantly at
Paw-Paw. "Now what do you have for me, Mrs. Low?"

Self-consciously, Paw-Paw put her hands up by her collar,
lifting the chain until the charm appeared outside.

"Oh, my," said the director, rising from his seat. "Oh, yes." Supporting himself on his arms, he leaned across the desk. "Exquisite. Simply exquisite. I've never seen jade of this quality and the lines, simple yet powerful."

"This charm, it's been in our family for years," Paw-Paw said.

"What?" The director blinked and seemed to notice Paw-Paw again. "Oh, yes. You don't say. I can see it's very old." He sat back down again.

Paw-Paw let go of the chain so it rested just below her collar. "You must understand," Paw-Paw explained patiently, "that the owl charm has many memories for my family. What those memories are, I cannot say to a stranger; but there are many. We would not sell it if we had a choice and we will not sell it to you at all if we do not think it will be treated right."

The director sat back in his big leather chair. "Mrs. Low, let me assure you that this museum is noted for the quality of its displays. In our possession we have millions of dollars' worth of the world's art treasures that span the ages."

Paw-Paw pushed her glasses higher up on her nose the way she had when she had inspected the seams on the dress Pam-Pam had given me and pronounced the sewing very poor. "What other people do with their things is their business, but"—she covered the charm momentarily with her hand—"my family has only this one charm."

The director rested his elbows on the arms of his chair, pressing his fingertips together and thinking for a moment. Suddenly he disappeared behind his desk. We heard a heavy drawer being drawn out and the sounds of rummaging. The director reappeared the next moment with a large silver pocket watch in his hands. He placed it on the desk so we could see the unicorn delicately engraved on the silver lid. It had ruby eyes and an ivory horn, and when he flipped up the lid, we heard chimes ringing some pleasant melody.

"It isn't practical to wear this watch. A good many would prefer a self-winding Timex that can survive a ride in a washing machine. But there would be a number of people who would like it as a pretty decoration to add to their collection. And there would be a few, just a very few, who would appreciate it as the culmination of centuries of Swiss craftsmanship. Since I am the last of my family, no one else realizes that this was the one thing of value my great-grandfather carried around the Horn with him back in 1849 when he went to the California gold fields."

He looked down at the watch. "A museum can't really put sentiment on display, but it can and will try to make other people see that your charm was created by a great, imaginative man long ago and relate it to the works of other men of equally great imaginations. A work of art belongs to more than one person or family or nation but to all people." He raised his eyebrows inquiringly. "But if you have time, let me show you."

"We have time, but do you, Sherman?" Paw-Paw asked.

Sherman waved his hand with the cigar. "All the time you need, Mrs. Low."

"Good," grunted the director. He pressed a button on his intercom. "Miss Delacroix. Cancel my appointments for today with my regrets." He looked up with a smile like a boy getting out for summer vacation. "If they ask why, say I have some very important people with me today."

Two weeks later, while the Pachinko and I stood behind them, Mr. Jeh and Paw-Paw sat on the marble bench inside the museum. Paw-Paw rested her hands on the handle of her cane. She had to use one now because she limped and the doctor said she would always limp, and sometimes lately in the mornings, the cold would make her leg ache.

In front of us the line of people shuffled forward under the frosted white light past the display cases. There were a lot of things to see in the Asian wing of the museum, so that many people simply went on past the window where the charm nestled on blue velvet. But the people who did look at it nodded their heads in admiration.

The director folded his arms across his chest. "I know that some day your charm is going to be almost as popular as our bronze rhinoceros."

"That's good," Paw-Paw said politely. She did not care for most of the other exhibits. Over the centuries, Chinese art had gone through so many changes in style that the only kind of art Paw-Paw cared about was the stuff they made nowadays. But even so, Paw-Paw had appreciated the private tour that the director had taken us on. She may not have understood all the names of the dynasties and the fancy words and the different art styles, but she understood when someone was taking the time to share with us something he really valued. And I suppose, in a way, the collections in the museum were the personal creations of the director.

"The Broschats saw your charm's quality immediately and

were only too happy to donate the money," the director said.

"It was very kind of them," Paw-Paw murmured, taking pride as a young couple paused in front of the charm and spoke in low, admiring voices. "It's as you said," she whispered up to the director.

Art, though, wasn't to everybody's taste. The Pachinko looked bored but he kept his mouth shut. Ever since his great-uncle had saved him, he'd stopped trying to do the James Dean routine—I mean, like all of a sudden he'd found out that it wasn't just a game but that it could really get him killed. But when he had listened to the director as much as he could, he muttered something about going outside for a smoke and headed for the door.

"I need some fresh air," I said then. " 'Scuse me." He was already outside, balancing on the little wall around the long, rectangular pool in front of the museum. Lily pads covered most of the surface of the pool except for one large moss-covered rock where a bronze statue of Pan played on his pipes and stared at a clump of reeds. The Pachinko took out a pack of Winstons, shook out a cigarette, and planted it dangling between his lips while he got out his matchbook. He started to light it one-handed but the breeze was blowing too strong and the match went out. He tried five more times. His face took on an intense, studious expression like cigarette smokers get sometimes when they're having trouble lighting up.

"I thought you took the charm and all that time you were really trying to get it back for us," I said. "I'm sorry."

"It's okay. You were in good company when you suspected me." He went on trying to light up.

"Here," I said. "Stand this way." I jumped up beside him on the little wall around the pond. He turned around to face me so his back was to the wind and then he bent forward a little, using both hands to strike the match between my hands, which I cupped before him.

"Five to three, you sent us the five dollars each week, didn't you?"

The Pachinko shook his match out and was going to flip it into the pool when he saw the cop watching us. So instead he licked his thumb and forefinger and pinched out the match head. The match hissed as it cooled off instantly and he stuck the match in his pocket. "I get a lot of tips so I thought I'd share my luck around."

We'd gotten four envelopes since I found out it wasn't Barney.

I dug my hand into the pocket of my coat and handed all four of them over to him still unopened. "I didn't ask you for these."

Gilbert stared at them unhappily. "I know. I know. But what's the harm in taking them?" He tried to hand them back to me.

I stuffed my hands inside my coat pockets and stepped back from him. "I'll just tear them up," I warned him.

He tapped the envelopes against his leg. "Two to one you would at that."

"Make that a hundred to one."

With a sigh he stowed them away in one of his rear pants pockets. "My money's not good enough, huh?"

With my hands still in my coat pockets, I flapped the sides of my coat. "How do you think we'll feel the day we hear you've been found facedown in some alley?"

"Christ," the Pachinko said, "now don't you start on me too. Uncle has been riding my tail ever since he helped me out in that fight."

"Helped you? He saved you. Did you ever think he might be right? You might not be as tough as you think you are."

The Pachinko leaped down from the little wall. "Hey, what gives? Did I spit in your beer or something? Why are you riding me too?"

"You could jump in that pool for all I care," I snapped back. "It's just that you put on this act and I bet you don't even like it. You just like what people do when you put on that act." I started to walk away from him, balancing along the wall. After a moment, I heard the Pachinko keeping pace on the ground beside me, his long, narrow, pointed shoes with the taps clicking on the pavement.

"You know what I like about your grandmom?" he asked finally. "You don't have to put on an act to impress her. You can just be what you are." When he stopped, I stopped.

"Yeah, but you used to put on your act even when you were around her."

He jumped back up on the wall ahead of me. "So I got a public."

"How come you haven't been doing your act lately?"

He shrugged. "So maybe it's time to retire. A guy's only got so much luck, you know."

"Your uncle will probably rub it in for a while."

"What will *you* feel?"

I brushed my hair back from my mouth. "I'll feel smug."

Gilbert stared at our reflections in the pool. Suddenly he smiled lopsidedly and exhaled the smoke in one long, slow streamer. "I knew there was some reason why I liked you. You're like your grandmom."

The museum looked down on a little valley where a regular outdoor theater had been built in a grove of trees. The trees were old and gnarled and there were big ugly knobs, I guess where the tree had been pruned, but the leaves were beginning to shoot out—like tiny little flames of green—as though spring were burning up the trees.

"What will you do?"

"Oh, I don't know. I'm pretty good with cars. Maybe I'll get a job as a grease monkey in some garage."

Gilbert rocked back and forth on his heels. "Anyway, what do you say about letting me treat you and your grandmom to dinner once a week? At least I'll know you get one decent meal."

"You don't have to do that."

"I don't get much conversation from a restaurant wall. That's how I usually take my meals. It'd be a favor to me, Casey."

It was my turn to stare down at our reflections. For one moment, they seemed so clear and perfect, like our real selves were down there underneath the water, and the surface of the pool was just a sheet of glass; and then a water bug skittered over the surface, sending slight ripples across the pool, distorting our reflections. I smiled up at Gilbert. "I guess. Why not?"

IV

GILBERT dropped us off at Paw-Paw's place with the understanding that he and his great-uncle would pick us up late for dinner. Paw-Paw and I didn't talk too much until after we had the teapot in the middle of the table with the jasmine tea filling the room with the scent of springtime and the drowsy afternoon sunlight glowing softly in the narrow alley outside. I heard the other people starting to come home, their voices growing in number and volume, and they didn't sound strange to me at all. Instead, it was reassuring like the surging of the sea at high tide, rising louder and higher.

Both Paw-Paw and I kicked off our shoes and put on our Chinese slippers—I had my own pair now, they were so cheap. I crossed my legs and wriggled my foot, letting the slipper slap against my heel rhythmically.

"I told Gilbert to stop giving us the money," I said. "He won't anymore."

"That's good."

"He's thinking about quitting driving the car and getting a garage job instead."

"I hope so for his sake." Paw-Paw took a chopstick and, lifting the lid, stirred the tea inside the teapot, trying to get the tea properly steeped. "Why didn't you talk to Barney this morning when he called?"

"Even if I could forgive him for hurting you, he made you sell the charm."

"His life was more important than an old rock—even if the rock was carved in a nice way." Paw-Paw took the chopstick out, tapping it on the rim of the teapot lightly to shake off the drops. "And he's done like he said. He's joined a program that helps people who want to stop gambling."

"But the charm was so beautiful," I protested.

Paw-Paw replaced the lid and lifted the pot up by its handle, keeping the fingers of her free hand on the lid so it wouldn't fall off. Out of the spout poured a smooth pencil of amber tea, first into one cup and then into the other. "It's a funny thing about that. I looked and I looked at that old rock today and it didn't look half as nice as I remembered it." She set the teapot back on the table and placed a cup before me. The pink cup was of heavy restaurant porcelain.

"But if you're not wearing it, will that pretty green color fade away again?"

"I think it will stay green," Paw-Paw said.

And I thought to myself, I didn't have to be just like a Chinese owl. I could be like an American one too—I mean, I could be as wise as an American owl—I already felt a lot older and wiser than anyone else my age. I put my elbows on the table, nursing the teacup between the fingertips of both my hands. At first I only let myself sniff at the jasmine tea, knowing that the tea is never sweeter than just before the first taste. And finally I sipped it, knowing that spring was here.

When I finished my tea, I set my teacup down with a little porcelain clink. "Do you mind if I phone Barney? I want to wish him good luck. He'll need the encouragement."

"Do what you like." Paw-Paw slid the rubber band from around her deck of cards.

The mattress gave underneath me as I sat down on the bed and began to dial the telephone.

I recognized Morey's deep, rich voice when he answered the pay telephone in the hotel hall. "Casey, is that you?"

"Morey"—I fiddled with the phone cord—"how've you been? You got any gigs right now?"

"I'd have to use a comb and tissue paper."

"Morey," I scolded him, "you hocked your horn again."

"That's jes for a little while, baby."

"Did you do it for Barney?"

"Oh, no, baby. Man's gotta step out ev'ry now and then. Wanted to get my suit out so I traded the man even steven. Ole Morey was jes goin' to trade his suit back for his horn when you called."

"Is Barney there? Could I speak to him."

"Sure, baby. Sure." Morey suddenly sounded happy. "You jes wait a sec." Morey cupped his hand over the receiver but I could still hear him shout for Barney. Other people in the hall picked it up the way they will, carrying the announcement through the hotel until they find the person or find out where he or she is.

I glanced back at the window. One by one, the lights in the apartments were going on, blending with the warm red light of the setting sun. Paw-Paw had set the cards out on the table for a game of solitaire but the light was failing too fast. She leaned forward, squinting at the cards. "Your queen, Paw-Paw. Put the queen on the king. Over there to your right." I leaned over the headboard to flip on the light and as I did so, I heard Paw-Paw slap a card down.

And then Barney was on the phone. "Hi, Barney. How ya been?"

Connected
Readings

from Thief of Hearts

Laurence Yep

Approximately two decades after Child of the Owl, *everything is going well for Stacy (Casey's daughter). She's part of a loving family, popular at school, and gets good grades. But then a family from China moves into the area, along with their daughter, Hong Ch'un. Forced together, the two develop an instant dislike for each other. Unfortunately, Stacy is expected to show Hong Ch'un around school. Taking the other girl to the vice-principal's office, Stacy hopes to get rid of her there.*

MR. BARROWS, the vice-principal, was a balding, middle-aged man with wire-rim glasses. He always gave the impression of being an incomplete picture because there was always something untidy about him—either his shirttail was hanging loose or his shoelaces were untied.

"Well, your records are most impressive," he said to Hong Ch'un, consulting a file. "We have some evaluative tests for you to take, but in the meantime you can go to class with Stacy so you can get acclimated."

That was the last thing I needed. "Some of my classes are advanced ones. They may be pretty hard for a newcomer, sir."

"I can keep up," Hong Ch'un insisted.

Mr. Barrows smiled at me. "I know Stacy will make you feel comfortable. Did you bring a combination lock, Hong Ch'un?"

When Hong Ch'un shook her head, Mr. Barrows closed the file. "Do you know what one is?"

Hong Ch'un stiffened. "Of course."

He smiled apologetically. "You can get one at any hardware store. In the meantime, maybe Stacy will share her locker with you."

Hong Ch'un stood where she was. She was as keen about the notion as I was. "It isn't necessary."

"Nonsense." Mr. Barrows smiled. "You don't mind, do you, Stacy?"

"It isn't necessary," Hong Ch'un repeated.

With a shrug, Mr. Barrows shoved a sheet of paper toward her. "Well, here's your list of room assignments. Just follow Stacy."

"It isn't necessary."

Mr. Barrows glanced at her and then at me. "Is there some problem I don't know about?"

"I don't need help," Hong Ch'un said, and glared at me. Actually she meant she didn't want *my* help.

"What have I done to you?" I asked.

"My father ordered me to be nice to you," she said.

"Thank you for being very gracious," I said sarcastically.

Hong Ch'un, though, didn't realize I was joking. "Your father is a very good friend to mine." From her frown, she didn't relish the role.

"Don't do me any favors," I snapped.

She stiffened as if insulted. "You don't want my friendship? All Chinese are supposed to stick together."

"I don't call it friendship to badger me like you did in the car," I said.

"I know Hong Ch'un didn't mean anything," Mr. Barrows said quickly.

I shook my head. "We just don't get along, Mr. Barrows. I think you ought to get someone else to help her today."

"But you're the best person for the job," he insisted.

I pressed my hand against the skin below my throat. "Why?"

If Mr. Barrows had explained that I was good with newcomers, he might have won me over. Instead, he pressed his fingertips together and said, "Well, she is Chinese."

"So?" I asked. "I just met her this morning. I don't know her."

"You're both Chinese." Mr. Barrows could be as pigheaded as my mother. "That is, your mother is Chinese," he said. He knew her well from PTA meetings.

"Southern Chinese," I corrected him. "And Hong Ch'un is northern. We've got as much in common as you would with an African."

"I have been to Nigeria three times." Mr. Barrows indicated several photos on the wall. "I am proud to claim an African heritage. I'm surprised at you, Stacy."

All my life I thought I was just like everyone else. In fact, that's the way I still feel. So it was a shock to find out that people didn't share the same opinion.

"It's not fair to lump me in with her, sir," I said stubbornly. "You should pick me out for my abilities, not for the way I look. Would you want someone to ask you to do something on that basis?"

"I've picked you because you are the best possible choice for the job," he said firmly.

I felt cornered and that, in turn, made me feel frustrated.

"Why?" Tactically, it was a bad mistake.

"My grandmother was a teacher. My parents were both teachers. I tried to be a car salesman." From his suit pocket he pulled an old-fashioned fountain pen—the kind you had to fill up with ink. "I bet you think I carry this around because I'm too cheap to buy a new pen."

I rolled my eyes, because he found a way to tell this story to every student who wound up in his clutches.

Mr. Barrows fingered the pen affectionately. "This was my grandfather's. His first class gave it to him." The pride in his eyes was obvious as he set it down again. "I could no more avoid my vocation than my heritage."

I knew that the only way to avoid a longer lecture was to agree with him. "Yes, sir."

Outside his office, Hong Ch'un whirled. "I don't like being paired with a *t'ung chung,* either."

It was a term I had never heard Mom or Tai-Paw use. However, from her tone, I knew it was meant to be an insult. "A what?"

"So you're deaf, too." And she used the name again before she stalked away, much to my relief.

At that moment I felt a tap on my shoulder. "I thought we were supposed to ride to school together."

I turned to see Karen. "It was my parents' idea to go to school with that new girl, Hong Ch'un. They sprang it on me at the last moment so I couldn't tell you. Sorry."

"It's okay." She shrugged. "Would you like to do some homework together?" She continued in a small voice, "Like in the old days?" I was going to tell her no, but she added, "You haven't come to visit me in a long time."

"I do all the time," I said.

She shook her head. "You used to."

I tried to remember the last time I had visited Karen at night—any night—and realized that I couldn't. It wasn't intentional. I'd simply gotten involved in all different kinds of activities. Maybe I took her for granted as much I did Tai-Paw.

All right, she was a little odd—but not very much if you considered her parents. And she was so sweet and helpful that I didn't want to hurt her feelings any more than I already had. "How about tomorrow?" I suggested.

"What about tonight?" she asked.

"I have to appease the parental units and baby-sit Hong Ch'un and her family." I sighed.

"It's okay," Karen said, but she looked disappointed.

But it wasn't okay with me. "I'll make it up to you sometime," I promised.

"Sure," Karen said doubtfully.

However, in our first class, the teacher, Mr. Arnold, made Karen move her seat.

I glanced at Karen. We hadn't made any trouble. (All right, so maybe we did talk a little and giggle a little; but is that a crime?)

"I want you to help our new classmate adjust," said Mr. Arnold. He turned to address the class. "Hong Ch'un has just arrived from China. Mr. Barrows said from Beijing, in fact." When he glanced at her, she nodded confirmation. Motioning for her to take a seat, Mr. Arnold headed toward the front of the classroom. "Stacy, will you share your textbook with Hong Ch'un?"

From the look of distaste on her face, Hong Ch'un didn't like the idea any more than I did.

Karen already had her things in her arms and got up. "Have fun," she muttered.

"I won't," I said as I slumped in my chair. Suddenly I felt like I was in Sylvia's movie; I could understand the impulse to kill an unwanted twin.

In the next class that morning, Ms. Armstrong also made sure I sat next to Hong Ch'un so I could share my books with her and help her adjust. It made me feel as if I were under a curse for the rest of the morning.

On the way to our next class, Jeff clapped a hand on my shoulder. "Why so glum, chum?"

"The teachers keep sticking me with the pickle of all pickles," I said.

"She's not very nice," Karen said from behind us.

Jeff ignored Karen, the way most kids did at Merc. In fact, most of them didn't know who she was if I mentioned her name. It was as if she were the Invisible Girl.

I made a point of smiling at her. "You got that right."

Jeff barely glanced at her as he reached into his backpack with a confident grin. "Dr. Sunshine to the rescue." But after a moment the grin became a grimace as he began to rummage around frantically in his bag. Finally he opened the flap and began taking out books, notepads, and other interesting junk, including one old knitting needle. "My toy's gone."

Sylvia combed her hair from her face with her hands. "Cheer up. It's bound to turn up."

Jeff glumly shook his now-empty backpack over the concrete path.

He flung the bag down in disgust. "It reminded me of a toy I had when I was a kid." He slapped his forehead. "I told Cindy that, when I saw it in the store window, and she got it for me. She's gonna kill me."

"Maybe you can buy another to replace it," I suggested sympathetically.

He tapped his pockets. "No dinero."

Beneath all of Jeff's wackiness was a genuine desire to make people happy. I realized with a start that Jeff had been my friend almost as long as Karen. I took him for granted too. "I'll loan you the money."

"You will?" he asked in surprise.

I started to reach for my wallet. "How much?"

He thought about it for a moment and then began to stuff his things back into his pack. "Naw, I couldn't. It doesn't seem right to borrow money from one girl to replace a present bought by another girl."

"And Cindy would hound you beyond the grave if she found out," Sylvia added.

Jeff anxiously sprang to his feet. "You're not going to tell, are you?"

"What's it worth to you?" Sylvia asked as we began walking again to our next class.

"I told you I don't have any money," Jeff protested.

"Fine, you can pay me back in services." Sylvia began to tick off the items on her fingers. "You can mow our lawn and . . ."

As she listed the items, Jeff groaned. "This is extortion."

"No, extortion is where I threaten to break your legs if you don't mow my lawn." Sylvia batted her eyelashes in mock flirtation. "The proper term for what I'm doing to you is *blackmail*."

However, it was Sylvia's turn to panic in government class when Ms. Sims announced a surprise quiz.

I had been paired yet again with Hong Ch'un, so I didn't notice Sylvia at first. Suddenly there was a cascade of clunks behind me. I turned to see that Sylvia had overturned her bag. Books, pens, and lipstick spilled off the desktop onto the floor. "I can't find my rabbit's foot."

"You had it this morning," I said.

Sylvia squatted down, fingers splayed outward as she swept her hands over the linoleum. "It's got to be here somewhere. Help me look."

Ms. Sims was coming over. "You can buy another after school," I said.

Sylvia straightened up with a wail. "But the test is now."

Jeff touched Sylvia's shoulder. "Come on. Get back in your seat."

Sylvia shot up and grabbed his vest. "If you stole it, Jeff . . ."

Jeff shoved her away. "I'm not that desperate."

Ms. Sims loomed over Sylvia. "Put that trash away and get ready for the test."

I slipped out of my desk and knelt beside Sylvia, who shot a grateful look at me. "Can you believe that Jeff? I bet he's trying to weasel out of our deal."

"It'll turn up," I tried to reassure her. She'd probably find her lucky charm in another pocket, and the windup kangaroo had probably fallen out of Jeff's backpack.

Sylvia slapped the linoleum miserably. "You can't trust anyone these days."

After we had passed the completed quizzes forward, I looked behind me toward Sylvia. Mutely she shook her head and then, resting her elbows on the desktop, buried her face against her arms.

People lose little things every day, and at first I assigned the losses to coincidence. But then Mr. Barrows came on the public address system.

"Fun is fun," declared Mr. Barrows, sounding too annoyed to enjoy what might be a joke. "But will the person or persons who stole my pen return it to me? It has little monetary value, but it is worth an immense amount in sentiment. Whoever has stolen it has taken a little bit of my heart. If the pen is left in my box, I will not ask any questions."

Everyone started to chuckle because at some time we all had heard the story about the pen. Mr. Barrows used it to make a point on everything but the law of gravity.

However, everyone sobered up when Mr. Barrows added, "If this polite request is not honored, I will have to take more forceful measures."

Instantly people turned around to stare at Jeff, because he was always playing pranks. Helplessly he placed his hands upon his chest. "I didn't take it. For once, I'm innocent."

Sylvia looked up from her desk. "Maybe I didn't lose my rabbit's foot. Maybe somebody took it."

"And my windup toy," Jeff said.

"Unless," Sylvia said darkly, "you staged the theft to throw off suspicion."

"Jeff's jokes are never mean," I said to her. "But these thefts are just plain malicious."

Jeff nodded. "They may seem like nothing, but the things that were stolen were important to the owners."

"Who knew about the toy?" Sylvia demanded.

"I was playing with it most of the morning." Jeff shrugged. "So it'd be just about everybody."

Sylvia sighed. "Everyone knows about my rabbit's foot."

"You too?" another girl asked. "I lost one of my piano earrings." She indicated a cheap plastic hoop. "They were a souvenir of my visit to the Liberace Museum."

Mr. Barrow's announcement made other people compare their losses. They were all silly things—a ribbon, a sticker on a binder. It was nothing you could go to the police about. The monetary value was probably less than five bucks; but you couldn't put a price tag on the sentimental value.

If Jeff hadn't lost his toy, I would have said he was the likely culprit, but he had been just as upset as Sylvia. I sympathized with him, of course, just as I did with Sylvia and my other friends who had lost their treasures. At the start of lunch period, I even said something to Mr. Barrows about his loss.

"I can't understand," he complained to me. "It's not worth anything." He held out a hand to me. "Stacy, everyone in the school listens to you. Spread the word. If this is a joke, it isn't funny. I just want my pen back."

I felt sorry for Mr. Barrows. "I will," I promised, but it would have to be tomorrow. Today I was more nervous about having to entertain Hong Ch'un. As a result, though the whole campus was buzzing about the thefts, I decided to try to patch up things with Hong Ch'un over lunch.

When the bell rang, Karen asked me her usual question: "So where do you want to have lunch?"

I made a point of including Hong Ch'un. "Where would you like to eat, Hong Ch'un?" I asked her.

Hong Ch'un seemed surprised by the invitation. Almost shyly she said, "Somewhere where it's green."

"We could sit under the oak tree," I suggested. "That way we could have shade."

On the lawn in front of the school was an old tree even older than Merc itself. It had huge roots, and its branches were as thick as my waist.

From her lunch bag, Hong Ch'un pulled one of those cruller-like Chinese doughnuts that are really salty. And in her other hand she had a fat, squat little plastic thermos of what I thought was tea until she dipped the doughnut into it and took a bite.

When I glanced into the thermos I saw that it held homemade rice porridge. "Having *jook*?" I asked conversationally.

"We call rice porridge *chu*," she corrected me.

"Well, we call it *jook*," I explained. I thought my mother's dialect was just as good as hers. "Did they have many trees where you lived?"

"I lived in the heart of the city." She swirled the doughnut around in the porridge. "If I wanted trees, I went to the park. I like climbing."

"There used to be trees all around here, but now they're mostly gone. But when I was a kid, I was a regular squirrel." I grinned weakly at her. She said nothing, but she had a thoughtful look, as if she were searching for something else to say and keep the conversation going. So I knew that I had made contact somehow.

She sampled my lunch, but she shared my opinion that Dad had made rabbit's food. Throughout lunch, Karen kept eating steadily. Hong Ch'un's eyes widened when she saw Karen begin to eat a second fat sandwich. "You shouldn't eat so much," Hong Ch'un scolded. "It isn't good for you."

Karen deliberately crammed half of the sandwich into her mouth. "You need lessons in being polite."

I tried to smooth things over. "She comes from a different culture with different customs."

Karen looked at me with those hurt, puppy-dog eyes of hers. "She's in America now, so she ought to learn some American manners—just like she shouldn't wear kiddy barrettes in her hair."

Hong Ch'un's hand shot up to one of her Snoopy barrettes. "What's wrong with these?"

Karen was normally very sweet unless you hurt her feelings. "They're only for five-year-olds."

"That's rude, Karen," I said. "You can't make fun of her just because she doesn't know our fashions." I sounded just like my mother.

With an angry look at me, Karen got up. "Well, she started it."

"Don't go away mad," I coaxed.

"I don't like the company you keep," she said over her shoulder, and walked away.

Hong Ch'un closed a hand around one of her pigtails. "I wish you had told me."

"Sorry. I meant to tell you later," I said, crunching through another mouthful of lettuce. "I've got some rubber bands you could use."

Hong Ch'un hesitated and then dropped her hand. "No, I'll wear these for today," she said with dignity.

I capped my Tupperware. "Tell you what. Let's go to a rest room and I'll help you do your hair."

Hong Ch'un held on to one braid. "I suppose over here the barrettes are probably very cheap. But they were a gift from my grandmother. She heard that was what American girls wore over here. She obtained them with great difficulty because we were still in China."

"How did your grandmother get the barrettes?" I asked kindly.

"I don't know," Hong Ch'un said. "But things come in from Hong Kong and find their way to Beijing."

I felt bad for Hong Ch'un, and a little ashamed that I had felt superior to her about her wearing them. "I'm sorry."

"You're lucky to have your Tai-Paw," Hong Ch'un said wistfully and added, "I'm sorry too. Things are so different here. I don't mean to say the wrong things."

She wasn't so bad when she bent a little. "You'll learn," I said.

She looked away. "Sometimes I feel so lost. Father says I must change, but if I do, I think I will get even more lost."

"I guess it would be scary," I agreed.

Her head dipped slightly. "And this morning I met you: You don't want to have anything to do with what I value most. And if someone like you thinks that way, how will the others think?"

And I thought that *she* had been the one acting superior. Maybe it was both of us. I had a lot to think about as we headed back to the lockers. There was a crowd around the lockers, including Karen, but when I tried to say hello to her, she merely glared. She still didn't forgive me.

With a sigh, I squatted down before my locker and opened it. "May I?" Hong Ch'un asked, and when I got out of the way, she took out her small backpack. As she lifted it up, something fell with a clink on the linoleum.

"You dropped something." Karen swiftly stooped and retrieved the object.

"Wait." I took it from Karen's hand. "Where did you get this?" I demanded from Hong Ch'un.

Hong Ch'un looked down at her backpack, bewildered. "I don't know."

I held up the object so everyone could see it. It was Mr. Barrows's pen. "I did not take it," she declared. "I did not take it."

Sylvia, who had the locker next to ours, snatched the backpack from Hong Ch'un. "That's mine!" Hong Ch'un cried.

Before Hong Ch'un could stop her, Sylvia had thrust a hand inside and pulled out a windup kangaroo. "Anybody recognize this?"

Jeff pushed his way through the gathering crowd. "Hey, that's my toy!"

Sylvia produced a rabbit's foot from the backpack. "So what's my lucky charm doing here?"

The crowd closed in at that point as others began going through the backpack. Hong Ch'un backed away until she bumped into the lockers.

I went over to her urgently. "How did that stuff get into your backpack?"

Hong Ch'un huddled into herself, shoulders raised, elbows tight against her sides. "I do not know. Someone must have put them there."

"Are you accusing me?" I asked.

She stiffened indignantly. "You are not saying *I* did it?"

"Who else?" demanded Sylvia. "It was your backpack."

"No, no! Please! You have to believe me!" She looked at the others. "I am no thief!" She got so excited that her thoughts got ahead of her tongue, and she began to speak in Chinese rather than in English.

Karen planted a fist on her hip. "Stacy, what kind of person is your new friend?"

"I am no thief," Hong Ch'un insisted, backing down the hallway. We watched her dart away until she turned the corner.

"There has to be an explanation for this," I said. "Hong Ch'un might lack tact, but she's no thief."

"Why did she run if she was innocent?" Sylvia was rubbing some dirt from her rabbit's foot.

"After all, the loot was in her bag," Jeff pointed out. "What more proof do you need?"

"I still think we ought to get her side of it," I argued. "In civics, they say you're supposed to be innocent until proven guilty."

Exasperated, Sylvia spread her arms. "You should be the last one to defend her. Because if it isn't her, then it has to be you. The stuff was in your locker."

"I don't need your lucky charm," I said.

"Well," Sylvia admitted, "I guess I can see why you'd side with her."

"What do you mean by that?" I demanded indignantly.

Sylvia jabbed her rabbit's foot at me. "I never thought of you as being Chinese . . . until now."

"What's that got to do with it?" I demanded.

"Why else are you defending her?" Sylvia shrugged. "I thought you were my friend. If she were anyone else, you'd think she was guilty too. But you're taking the side of a perfect stranger against me—just because she's Chinese like you."

I felt . . . well . . . insulted—though I shouldn't have. It wasn't because I thought there was something wrong with China. It's just that I didn't like being called different. "I'm just like you," I insisted.

Despite the recovery of the rabbit's foot, Sylvia was still feeling upset. "You just proved you aren't. Or you'd know who your friends are and who the thieves are."

I had grown up with Sylvia and had known her since second grade. All that time I thought she had considered me her equal. It was a shock to find out that Sylvia might think otherwise now.

I started to turn away. "In America, you get a fair trial no matter what you are."

Behind me, I heard a boy mutter to someone else, "See? She really is a half-breed or she wouldn't be trying to help that thief."

At some other time, I might have ignored the insult; but Sylvia's accusations had already made me feel like I was an outsider. Furious now, I whirled around. "Who said that?"

The nearest boy held up his hands. "It wasn't me."

"Whoever said that was a jerk," Jeff said. "Don't pay him any attention."

However, now that the words had been spoken, they could never be taken back because the damage had been done.

I knew almost everyone there. Quite a few had even gone to elementary school with me. Looking around at the other faces now, I wondered just how many thought that way even though they hadn't said so. Was anyone really my friend? Could I trust anyone again?

"Where are you going, Stacy?" Karen asked in her sad little voice. "Your class is in the other direction."

"I've got to find out something first," I said. Clenching the pen in my fist, I walked away, my strides getting wider and wider and faster and faster. Karen caught up with me.

"I think you need a friend," she said as she panted to keep up with me.

I smiled my thanks at her. Good old Karen was one person I could count on.

As we headed for the lockers of the Dumpster crew, I felt as if I had stepped over the border into a strange new world. It looked like my old one, but when I looked at details, there were things wrong with it.

I kept turning the scene over and over in my mind, and it made me feel ashamed, though there was nothing to be ashamed of. All the way across campus, I felt like kids were whispering and pointing at me like I had escaped from some freak show. Anytime anyone laughed, I even thought it was because of me. With those kinds of suspicions I'd go crazy in no time.

The Dumpster crew was still by their lockers, so I walked straight up to Victor Li. "What's *t'ung chung?*" I repeated the words Hong Ch'un had used for me.

"What?" he asked, puzzled.

When I told Victor again, he nodded his head. "Oh, you mean *t'ung chung,*" he said, correcting the tones. "Who said that?"

"Never mind. What does it mean?" I demanded.

Dwight Whang folded his arms smugly. "You think you are one big person. You think you are so good—too good for us."

I was surprised by that. "Whatever gave you that impression?"

"You walk around just like one of these." He waved a hand at some passing white students. "But you are not them. You are not us."

Victor punched Dwight in the arm. "Shut up."

I thrust an arm in between Victor and Dwight. "I want to know," I said to Dwight.

"You don't want to know. Go back to your friends," Victor urged.

I looked at my small, distorted reflection on the lenses of his glasses.

"What does it mean?"

"It means 'mixed seed,' " Dwight translated with satisfaction.

"That's literally," Victor said, trying to be helpful. "But it really means—"

"I know what it means." I lowered my arm. "In English it's half-breed. Is it as much an insult in Chinese as it is in English?"

"More," Victor said. "I'm sorry."

"Aren't we all sorry?" I said, and turned away.

Voices

Lucha Corpi

My father taught me to sing
my mother to spin verses
and from my grandmother I learned
that truth can be found
through silence as well

There are so many voices in me
so many voices going down
to drink at dreams' edge
on winter nights

Grandma Thinks I'm Beautiful

Peg Kehret

*Grandma Thinks I'm Beautiful is an example of a mono-
logue. Monologues are speeches delivered by a single character. Some monologues appear in a full-length play. Others,
like* Grandma Thinks I'm Beautiful, *are written to be read
by themselves or performed alone.*

MY grandma thinks I am beautiful. She can look straight at
my flabby thighs and my frizzed hair and my knobby knees and
still believe I'm the most gorgeous person alive.

Sometimes I tease her about it. I say, "Grandma, is something wrong with your eyesight? Have you had your glasses
checked recently? There are two huge pimples on my nose,
glowing like red lanterns. My ears are completely out of propor-
tion to the rest of my head; they look like a pair of deformed
mushrooms growing from the sides of my face. I would let my
hair grow out to cover my ears except every hair on my head
has a split end."

And do you know how she responds? Grandma laughs and
says, "To me, you are beautiful. And don't you ever forget it."

Secretly, I'm glad that she has never let me talk her out of
her opinion. It's comforting to know that no matter how ugly I
am to the rest of the world, there's at least one person who
thinks I look great. The funny thing is, when I'm with her, I *feel*
more beautiful. I stand up straighter and keep my hair combed
and wear clean clothes. Since she believes so hard that I am
beautiful, I feel an obligation to at least try to live up to her
expectations.

It isn't just my looks that Grandma applauds. It's everything
about me. She says I'm smart. She's constantly amazed at the
clever things I do. According to Grandma, I am well ahead of
any other kid my age in reasoning ability, athletic skill and con-
versational artistry. To say nothing of my musical talent.

The truth is, I am average. I'm good at some things, not so
good at others. If they had a universal curve for kids, overall I
guess I'd place right about in the middle. Grandma would never
admit that for a minute. She has always believed, and no doubt
will continue to believe, that I'm right off the charts. Top dog.

The genius kid of all time whose sterling character and sparkling personality match her sensational IQ.

Amazingly, she doesn't brag about me to her friends. Maybe she's afraid that if she started in on how clever I am, they would all want equal time to talk about their grandchildren.

She doesn't need to tell anyone else how she feels about me. The important thing is that she always lets *me* know how special I am: How bright and funny. How kind and fair. How honest and courageous. How beautiful.

Sometimes when I feel lazy and don't want to do my best at a difficult task, I think about Grandma and I try a bit harder. If I'm tempted to say something mean, I remember how good it feels to get a compliment, so I say something nice instead. When I think how proud Grandma will be if I do well in school, I'm never tempted to cheat or skip a test or neglect my homework. When you have a first-rate cheering squad, it makes you want to win the game. I don't ever want Grandma to be disappointed in me or ashamed of anything I do.

Every kid—and every adult—should have someone in their life who thinks they're beautiful. Most people would accomplish more and be happier, as well, if they could have my grandma, or someone like her, who firmly believes that they are wonderful and smart and kind.

Although I tease her about her eyesight and tell her she is hallucinating, I'm glad my grandma thinks I am beautiful.

I think she's beautiful, too.

Where Is My Country?

Nellie Wong

Where is my country?
Where does it lie?

The 4th of July approaches
and I am asked for firecrackers.
Is it because of my skin color?
Surely not because
of my husband's name.

In these skyways
I dart in and out.
One store sells rich ice cream
and I pick bittersweet nuggets.

In the office someone asks me
to interpret Korean,
my own Cantonese netted
in steel, my own saliva.

Where is my country?
Where does it lie?

Tucked between boundaries
striated between dark dance floors
and whispering lanterns
smoking of indistinguishable features?

Salted in Mexico
where a policeman speaks to me in Spanish?
In the voice of a Chinese grocer
who asks if I am Filipino?

Channeled in the white businessman
who discovers that I do not sound Chinese?
Garbled in a white woman
who tells me I speak perfect English?
Webbed in another
who tells me I speak with an accent?

Where is my country?
Where does it lie?

Now the dress designers flood us
with the Chinese look,
quilting our bodies in satin
stitching our eyes with silk.

Where is my country?
Where does it lie?

Take the World as It Is

Charles Swain

Take the world as it is!—with its smiles and its sorrow,
Its love and its friendship—its falsehood and truth—
Its schemes that depend on the breath of tomorrow!
Its hopes which pass by like the dreams of our youth—

Yet, oh! whilst the light of affection may shine,
The heart in itself hath a fountain of bliss!
In the *worst* there's some spark of a nature divine,
And the wisest and best *take the world as it is.*

New Day Dawning

Joyce Hansen

SARAH was careful of the thorns as she bent the stem of a deep red rose. She inhaled the flower's sweet perfume while watching several young men hurry through the gates and walk down the road. She knew that they were gone for good. Ever since the Yankee soldiers had come to the Thomas plantation in April to inform all of them that slavery and the war were over, people had been slowly leaving.

She picked another rose, turned around, and gazed toward the cotton fields, still dotted with the figures of men and women tending the growing plants that would be ready for picking by July. Sarah faced the road again and saw the young men disappear around a bend. In the past, the hounds would have chased them down, and Master George Thomas himself would have ridden, along with the patrollers, after them.

"Hey, girl, what're you looking after?"

Sarah jumped slightly. She hadn't heard Solomon approaching her. "Three more hands just left," she said.

"Yes. I know." A satisfied smile spread across his round face. "Ain't it wonderful? Them boys could just leave without a pass and see what's on the other side of this hill." His large eyes, as round as his face, fastened on her. "When are you leaving, Little Missy?"

"Don't call me that. I have a name." Sarah threw her head back and walked quickly toward the house.

Solomon followed her. "I'm just fooling with you, Sarah. Don't go getting mad."

Sarah passed the row of live oaks lining the walkway and glanced at Mistress Emmaline's bedroom window. Emmaline Thomas closed the curtain and moved away.

Solomon saw her, too. "Look at her watching her used-to-be property head down the road."

They walked toward the kitchen at the back of the house.

"What're you going to do?" Solomon asked.

"Don't keep bothering me. I don't know."

Sarah and Solomon were both fourteen years old and had been born into slavery on the plantation. No one, not even Solomon, who was like her brother, seemed to understand how

171

painful it was for Sarah to make a decision to leave the only life she'd known.

As she and Solomon entered the kitchen, the sweet smell of a pecan pie and Mariah's round scowling face greeted them. Mariah, the cook, was Solomon's mother and a mother to Sarah as well. Sarah's own mother had died giving birth to her.

"Where you been, Solomon? You might be free, boy, but you still have to work. Go on and fetch me some firewood." Her eyes fell on Sarah next. "You too, gal. No one's going to pay you to pick flowers."

"These are for Mistress."

Mariah sucked her teeth. "Mistress ain't studying you. Hardly talk to you or any of us since we been set free."

Davis, the Thomases' most favored slave, sat at the table as he did every morning, eating a piece of corn bread and drinking a cup of tea before beginning his chores.

He smiled at Sarah. "Little Missy, how're you this morning?"

Only Davis could call her that, for it never seemed as if he were mocking her. He had named her Little Missy when the Thomases' daughter, Caroline, had died at the age of ten. Sarah was a year older than Caroline and had been her slave and playmate. After her daughter's death, the grieving Emmaline Thomas increasingly sought Sarah's company. And the young girl became her mistress's personal slave and companion.

Sarah slept in Caroline's bedroom instead of on a pallet on the floor at the foot of Emmaline Thomas's bed.

"Mariah, I'm going to take these flowers to Mistress."

"Is she sick or something? You better stay here and learn how to cook, so you can support yourself. Cooks always find work."

Sarah sighed. "But Mistress might be wanting me."

"She knows where to find you if she wants you."

Sarah's small, brown, oval face, as well formed and delicate as the roses she carried, hardened like a little rock. Ignoring Mariah, who continued to grumble, she entered the sitting room. She'd spent some of the happiest times of her life here, playing with Caroline on the window seat as the sun filtered through the lace curtains, or sitting on the sofa next to Mistress Emmaline, learning how to make lace.

She put the roses in Mistress's favorite china vase, arranging the flowers as Mistress had taught her to do, and made up her mind to go upstairs without waiting to be sent for.

Mariah's voice broke into her thoughts. "Sarah, come on in here and help me."

Sarah ignored her and walked up the stairs. Before she reached the landing, Emmaline Thomas called from her bedroom. "Sarah, you mind Mariah."

"But, Mistress, I have some beautiful roses for you. Make you feel better."

"Go on and help Mariah."

Sarah's eyes stung as if she'd been slapped. More hurt than angry, she ran back down the stairs and put the vase on the fireplace mantel. Mistress knew how much she hated working in the kitchen.

Without a word, Mariah handed her a large basket of peas. Sarah placed the basket on her lap and sat near the window looking out onto the yard and the fields beyond. She listened for every sound in the house, hoping that Mistress would call her—wishing that their life could be the way it had been in the past.

Davis stared at her sympathetically. "Missy, you have to decide what you're going to do with this freedom." His teeth were as white and perfect as his starched shirt.

"I guess I'm going to set here and shell peas till my fingers fall off."

"You go on, Little Missy." He laughed.

"If she knows what I know she better leave with me and Solomon," Mariah said.

Sarah opened one of the pods so hard the peas popped out and rolled on the floor. "Mistress say that people who leave their homes are starving on the roads."

Mariah put her hands on her hips and bent over Sarah. "Girl, you'll be a slave all of your life."

"I am not a slave. Didn't Master and Mistress say they'll pay us wages?"

Mariah rolled her eyes. "Fifty cents a week? Even someone as ignorant as me knows that that ain't no money to build a future with."

"Well, Master and Mistress say—"

Mariah interrupted her. "Stop all that Master and Mistress slavery-time talk."

Davis drained his cup and smiled handsomely at Mariah.

"So what should the child call her? Emmaline?"

"Call her Miz Thomas and him Mister Thomas."

"Well, it seems strange to say something different," Davis said. "We been calling them Master and Mistress for so long. Maybe it don't mean nothing—just a way of addressing them."

"Names do mean something," Mariah insisted. "And Master

and Mistress mean slavery time."

Davis turned again to Sarah. "You didn't answer my question, Little Missy."

Sarah lowered her head over the peas as she tried fighting back panic and tears.

Mariah spoke to the top of Sarah's head.

"Sarah, I held you in my arms when you was a baby and your mother died. You are the same to me as Solomon, my own flesh. I held you in one arm and Solomon in the other. You won't ever have a new life if you stay here and live like you did in slavery. Come with us."

Sarah couldn't tell her that she never felt like a slave, especially when Mistress was teaching her how to make lace and to quilt and was even beginning to teach her how to draw.

"Sarah, me and Solomon are leaving for Charleston. There's a freedmen's school there. They even have black teachers from the North. It's wonderful to just think about! My son's going to learn how to read and write and I can get work as a cook and make more than fifty cents a week. I'm going to get some land, too." She plopped down in the chair as if the excitement of her plans had worn her out.

"I'm leaving too, Little Missy," Davis said. "Going to Virginia to find my son and his mother. They lived on the Williams farm and was sold away five years ago."

Sarah was so surprised that she found her voice. "You have a wife and child?"

She never realized that Davis had a life that went beyond serving George Thomas. He had been given as a wedding present to the Thomases when they'd married thirty years ago and Davis was ten years old. He was a reliable and faithful slave—as polished and tasteful as the Thomases' fine china and silverware. Davis, with his slight bows, knew how a table should be set, how a master should be dressed and a household should be run.

"It was a slave marriage," he explained. "But I'm going to find them, and we're going to have a real marriage by a priest."

"How do you know where to look?" Sarah asked, forgetting her own problems for a moment.

"I have the name of the family they was sold to in Richmond. I'll find them if I have to walk the whole state of Virginia."

"You see," Mariah said, and shook her finger in Sarah's face. "Nobody is staying. It's a new day dawning."

"But Master and Mistress always treated me good."

"They treated all of us good. They also treat their expensive furniture good. And treat their cows and horses good, too. Paid a lot of money for them, and for us, too. Would you abuse something you paid good money for?"

"We're not property now," Sarah said softly.

"That's the point. Old George and Emmaline don't own your hide no more. There's no reason to take good care of you. You are on your own. You better learn how to take good care of yourself."

"But Mistress said that the freed people are sleeping in the woods and eating wild berries, and starving to death."

"She also said that Yankees had tails and horns."

"But she's going to pay us wages and she's going to teach me how to paint."

"Girl, you remember when Caroline took it into her head to teach you how to read and write?" Mariah's face softened into a slight smile. "And then you decided to teach Solomon the two words you had learned, and Miz Thomas caught you? Gave you and Caroline a whipping and told her daughter it was against the law to teach a slave how to read and write. Do you remember that? Remember how you cried because you really wanted to learn?" She was silent for a moment. "If you stay here you'll never learn nothing except how to remain a good slave."

Before Sarah could answer, Solomon burst into the kitchen. "Hey, y'all, something's happening. Them hands all left the fields and is walking up to the house."

Davis stood up quickly, putting his arm around Solomon's shoulders. "Come on, son, let's look like you're helping me with a chore, so's we can find out why those hands are trooping off to the big house."

"Sarah? Sarah!" Mistress called from the sitting room.

"Well, she finally got out of that bedroom," Mariah mumbled, as she too headed for the yard to find out what was happening.

Sarah put the basket of peas on the table and rushed to the sitting room.

"Yes, Mistress?" Sarah said, and heard Mariah's voice in her head warning against slavery-time talk. "You want to walk in the garden?"

"No, I'm tired." The lines around her mouth were like two deep ditches.

Sarah pointed to the mantel. "I picked some roses for you."

Mistress did not look. Closing her eyes as if she were in pain, she asked, "Are you abandoning me, too?"

"No, Mistress."

Emmaline Thomas pushed a thin, gray strand of hair away from her forehead. "Sarah, don't try to fool me. Everybody has changed. Even Davis. How could he think of leaving us? I'm not surprised about Mariah. She always did have a mind of her own." Eyes still closed, she rocked back and forth slightly. "Why are they leaving, Sarah?"

"They're the same. They just . . . they just want to have a new life."

Emmaline Thomas frowned as though Sarah had said something foolish.

"What new life? They're leaving by ones and twos—a trickle, but one day, it's going to be a flood and they'll all be gone. But they'll be back here in a month, begging me and Master to take them in."

Nagged by the word *Master*, Sarah was silent.

"You know no other place but this one, Sarah. You'll end up living in some cabin with cracks in the ceiling, so that stars are looking down on you at night. You're not used to living like that."

Emmaline Thomas opened her eyes, and Sarah was shocked to see tears brimming on her lashes and then trickling down her wan cheeks. "Sarah, don't leave. Remember how you and Caroline used to play?"

The tears were painful for Sarah, bringing back a rush of memories of the days when Mistress and Caroline were her world. Tears welled up in her own eyes also.

George Thomas suddenly entered the room, his tall, bulky body dominating the space. "Emmaline!" he shouted excitedly. "The field hands are demanding that we put a school on the plantation, so their younguns can learn to read and write. If we don't do it, they'll leave us."

The flood has begun, thought Sarah.

Emmaline sat up. "What did you tell them?"

"I told them yes. I need those hands to bring in the crop, Emmy; otherwise, we'll lose everything. Oh, I'll open up the school for them. I'll even let that Freedmen's Bureau send one of them black northern teachers."

"Who's going to put up the school?"

"I'll supply the materials, and the hands will build it."

This was the first time that Sarah had seen George Thomas smile in a long while. He clutched his wife by her sagging shoulders.

"Oh, Emmy, if the hands stay, we can bring that cotton crop in and we won't lose everything. All they want is a school." He threw his large head back with its great mane of white hair, and laughed. "Emmy, you come on back to life. The world isn't dead yet."

He loosened his grip on her shoulders, and she gave him a weak smile. "Well, I don't suppose it'll do any harm. Those young ones are not much use in the field yet anyway."

Sarah didn't hear the rest of their conversation, for without warning, like a gift from heaven, the answer came to her, and she knew what she was going to do.

Emmaline Thomas's voice startled her out of her thoughts. "Come on, Sarah, let's take a walk, so I can see my garden."

As they strolled through the grounds bursting with roses and azaleas, Sarah asked, "If I stay here, am I free to go whenever I wish?"

"What kind of silly question is that? You belong here with us."

Sarah said nothing then or to Mariah and the others that evening. She wanted to make her decision strong in her own mind so that no one could change it. She could hardly fall asleep as she made her plans and strengthened her resolve.

She was up by dawn. She dressed quietly and sat on the side of her bed, waiting to hear her former mistress stirring. Finally, when she heard her walk across the room, Sarah knocked on the door and entered. "Miz Thomas, I have to talk to you."

Later, she ran down the stairs to tell the others the news. For a moment, though, when she saw Solomon, Davis, and Mariah sitting at the kitchen table, she felt as if her heart were splitting in two. "Morning, Little Missy," Davis said.

Sarah poured herself a cup of tea and sat down with them. "I made my plans," she said. "I told Miz Thomas that I would stay and work for her if I could go to the plantation school, too."

She braced herself for Mariah's eruption, but Mariah only asked quietly, "What did she say?"

"Said she didn't know why I wanted to learn to read and write; said it wasn't necessary for a colored girl to know such things. Said I already was a wonderful lady's maid. I told her that I wanted to be a teacher someday in a freedmen's school.

"And I told her I wouldn't abandon her if I could go to the plantation school. Then she said I could go to the school if I had a mind to."

Davis nodded his head. "You're growing up, Sarah. No more Little Missy, now."

"We can write each other," Solomon said.

Sarah looked at Mariah hopefully. "Now you can stay here, and Solomon can go with me to the plantation school."

But Mariah shook her round head. "Sarah, each of us takes freedom in his or her own way. I have to leave even if I only go around the bend to the Williams farm. If I stay here, I'll never feel free."

"That's right, Mariah," Davis agreed, tapping his forehead. "Freedom begins here, in our minds."

Sarah embraced each one of them. "Long as I'm free to go whenever I want, I don't mind staying a spell."

They were silent for a moment, listening to the whack of axes hitting the tree trunks as the bright sun burned off the last traces of morning darkness.

"Those hands have already started building their school-house," Davis remarked.

"There's a new day dawning for all of us," Sarah said, "former slaves and masters alike."

Prayer

Walter Dean Myers

Shout my name to the angels
Sing my song to the skies
Anoint my ears with wisdom
Let beauty fill my eyes

For I am dark and precious
And have such gifts to give
Sweet joy, sweet love,
Sweet laughter
Sweet wondrous life to live

i am kwakkoli

Bisco Hill

From *Merlyn's Pen: Fiction, Essays, and Poems by America's Teens*

Bisco Hill wrote this in the seventh grade. An avid sports fan, he loves to play football and baseball, with basketball being his favorite. In his school district, he was awarded the Boulder Optimist Citizenship Award for scholarship and citizenship.

A FEW months after my tenth birthday, my dad began to talk to me about receiving my Indian name. He said this had to be done in a ceremony by a medicine person or an elder in our tribe. My older sister, Megan, had received her Indian name, Maquegquay (Woman of the Woods), when she was only three. At that time my family lived on the Oneida Reservation just outside of Green Bay, Wisconsin. My grandfather was alive then, and he asked a medicine man friend of his to name her and made the arrangements. I always thought my sister's Indian name was so perfect for her. I was told the medicine man meditated for three days before the name came to him.

My family moved from Wisconsin to Colorado three years before I was born. My grandfather died when I was only two and a half, and both of these major events delayed my Naming Ceremony. My dad talked about naming me for several years, but it was hard to pull it together long distance. Because of the sacred and traditional aspects of this, it is not like anyone can just call and order a Naming Ceremony, like ordering a pizza! As it happened, my uncle Rick became the chairman of the tribe when I was ten, and he was able to talk to the right people and select the time. The right time was the summer solstice, near June 20, and it was also the time of the annual Strawberry Ceremony.

There are many traditions connected to the Naming Ceremony. For one thing, there are a limited number of names among the Oneida people. When a person dies, their name returns to the "pool" of available names and can be given to someone else. The medicine person decides whose energy fits which available name, or a person may ask for a certain name. In my case, I was named after my grandfather through my Anglo name, but I also wanted to take his Indian name which was available and had been waiting for

181

me for seven years. I felt that if I had both of his names, it made a full circle and I was wholly connected to him and to my family. The name that was his is "Kwakkoli," or "Whippoorwill" in English.

A few days before the ceremony in June of 1990, my parents and I flew to the Oneida Reservation. A friend of my dad made me a beautiful "ribbon shirt." It was a shade of deep turquoise stitched with pink, purple and green ribbons. My family and I thought it was very special and that I looked good in it.

Two days before I was given my Indian name, my uncle Rick, my dad and I drove around and looked at certain landmarks on the Oneida Reservation. I saw where my dad had grown up. There is a statue in the middle of the reservation of my great-grandmother, Dr. Rosa Minoka Hill. She was the first female Indian physician in the United States.

Oneida is very small and different from any other city I have known. It has only one school, several baseball fields, a small convent, a store, a post office, two churches, three cemeteries, a tribal building, and about twenty houses. My dad and his brother knew the names of everyone. They knew who was married to whom and who everyone's grandparents and parents were. They remembered all kinds of funny stories and laughed a lot. I thought it must be nice to live in a small town where everyone knows everyone for all those years. It is also a place where everyone is connected by common heritage, customs and beliefs.

The night before the ceremony, I got very nervous. My stomach hurt as if I had the flu, but I think it was just butterflies. I finally fell asleep about 3:30 in the morning. I don't know what I was afraid of—maybe just not knowing what was going to happen or what I would have to do. My mother could not come to the ceremony because only tribal members were allowed. We had just learned about this and I was upset that she couldn't come. She was disappointed, but told me to remember the details and tell her about it later.

After getting about four hours of sleep, I woke up to the sound of a shower running. I quickly put on my ribbon shirt, a pair of black pants and moccasins. The ceremony was set for 9:30 that morning, so we had to hurry.

On our short drive to the reservation, my stomach felt like it was going to explode! I had to at least get those butterflies flying in formation! I was pretty anxious, but really excited about getting my Indian name. We arrived at the longhouse a little early and I sat with my dad and one of his friends while other people finished setting up tables and chairs.

The ceremony finally began. The Faithkeeper called up the three clans of the Oneida Tribe: the Bear, the Turtle and the Wolf. I am in the Turtle Clan, so I would be named in the second group. The Faithkeeper named all the children in the Bear Clan, then moved on to the Turtles. He named two people, then stepped in front of me. He spoke to me in Oneida. It is a language with unusual sounds like no other language I have ever heard. Most of the words were not understandable to me. He later translated them as: "You must try to learn the Oneida language and our ways. I would like you to come to some of the other ceremonies and events. You now have an Oneida name, 'Kwakkoli,' and the Creator will know you by that name." I was proud to have both my grandfather's names because he was an important man in our tribe.

The Faithkeeper named the others and we all sat down as the Chief said a few more prayers. After about an hour, we all danced to Indian songs and drum music. It was fun, but became tiring after a while.

Next, we ate and drank. One of the drinks was a kind of strawberry juice. It is sacred and part of the ceremony because the Creator gave this gift of the strawberry to the Oneida people. The drink was very good.

When it was time to go, we thanked the Faithkeeper and the Chief and gave them gifts. The gift that I received, and will be mine for life, is a very special name that runs through my family and connects me to my grandfather, whom I barely knew. My name also reminds me of the many traditions and beliefs that are part of my heritage and about which I have a lot to learn and understand. I look forward to visiting my reservation as I grow up.

All Names Are American Names

Kie Ho

AT a recent seminar that my company sponsored, where many of the participants came from our overseas offices, a gentleman from the Netherlands looked at my name tag and said, "I see that you are from our division in California, but your name does not sound American." I told him that mine is indeed a Chinese name; however, I am an American citizen.

I should have told him that my name is as American as Lucille LeSueur or Margarita Carman Cansino before they became Joan Crawford and Rita Hayworth. My name does sound as foreign as the name of the Japanese slugger Sadaharu. Oh, but does it not also sound as American as Joe DiMaggio?

I have already simplified my name for Yankee ears. I was born Kie Liang Ho, which means Ho the First-Class Bridge. I skip the name Liang because it is so difficult for many to pronounce correctly. Even so, the short name has caused much confusion. Some secretaries write it as Keyhole. Others, deciding that such a short last name is impossible, change it arbitrarily to something more common, like Holm or Holt.

When I was sworn as an American citizen, I could have become Keith Ho, or Kenneth Ho, or even Don Ho. I decided to keep my Chinese name; this is one privilege that my new country gives me—the right to maintain my ethnic identity—and I cherish it.

Having a Chinese name does not necessarily mean that culturally I am a Chinese. I was born in Indonesia (which a lot of people misunderstand to be Indochina), and I do not write or speak Chinese. The only Chinese characters I can write are my name and my father's. Still, to everyone I am a Chinese. When somebody in my office has a birthday and we are all signing a card, people often say, "Come on, Kie, write something in Chinese." What I write is my dad's name, and I tell them that it means "Abundance of Fortune and Long Life." Actually, my father's name means Ho the Gold Fish.

Many people are confused by Asian names and nationalities. One day, my wife and I asked a patio contractor to give us a reference. He turned over page after page of his reference book and at last, with a friendly, victorious smile, he said, "Here you are, this one is a Chinese lady, Mrs. Nguyen." I hated to disappoint him by telling him that Nguyen is a Vietnamese name, and, since we do not speak Vietnamese at all, she might not be the best to call.

When our daughter was born, we did not give her a Chinese name. We thought that the name should be selected for the child, not for the parents' sake. We would have liked to name her May Hoa Ho, "Ho the Pretty Flower," but imagine the problems that she would face in school among children who like to make fun of "funny" names. So we gave her a "common" American name: Melanie. We hope that she will be as gentle as Melanie Wilkes in "Gone With the Wind." I wonder if Melanie Wilkes' mother ever knew that "Melanie" refers to something black: Would she still have named her so? Only Margaret Mitchell could tell.

So what's in a name? Benjamin Kubelsky changed his name (Jack Benny). Zbigniew Brzezinski did not. I will not, either.

A Nation of Nations

Senator Daniel Patrick Moynihan

THE Constitution of the United States begins: "We the People of the United States . . ." Yet, as we know, the United States is not made up of a single group of people. It is made up of many peoples. Immigrants from Europe, Asia, Africa, South America, and Australia settled in North America seeking a new life filled with opportunities unavailable in their homeland. Coming from many nations, they forged one nation and made it their own. More than 100 years ago, Walt Whitman expressed this perception of America as a melting pot: "Here is not merely a nation, but a teeming Nation of nations."

It was the ingenuity and acts of courage of these immigrants, our ancestors, that shaped the North American way of life. Yet, we sometimes take their contributions for granted. This fine series, *The Peoples of North America*, examines the experiences and contributions of the immigrants and how these contributions determined the future of the United States, Canada, and Mexico.

The immigrants did not abandon their ethnic traditions when they reached the shores of North America. Each ethnic group had its own customs and traditions, and each brought different experiences, accomplishments, skills, values, styles of dress, and tastes in food that lingered long after its arrival. Yet this profusion of differences created a singularity, or bond, among the immigrants. The poet Robert Frost put it well: "The land was ours before we were the land's."

The United States and Canada are unique in this respect. Whereas religious and ethnic differences sparked wars throughout the rest of the world—from the 17th-century religious wars to the 19th-century nationalist movements in Europe to the near extermination of the Jews under Nazi Germany—*we* learned to respect each other's differences and to live as one.

And the differences were as varied as the millions of immigrants who sought a new life in North America. In a mass migration, some 12 million immigrants passed through the waiting rooms of New York's Ellis Island; thousands more came to the West Coast. At first, these immigrants were welcomed because labor was needed to meet the demands of the Industrial Age.

Soon, however, the new immigrants faced the prejudice of earlier immigrants who saw them as a burden on the economy. Legislation was passed to limit immigration. The Chinese Exclusion Act of 1882 was among the first laws closing the doors to the promise of America. The Japanese were also effectively excluded by this law. In 1924, Congress established immigration quotas on a country-by-country basis.

Such prejudices might have erupted into war, as they did in Europe, but North Americans chose negotiation and compromise, instead. This determination to resolve differences peacefully has been the hallmark of the countries of North America.

The unique ability of Americans to live together as one people was seriously threatened by the issue of slavery. It was a symptom of a growing attitude of intolerance in the world. Thousands of English settlers had arrived in the colonies as indentured servants. These Englishmen agreed to work for a specified number of years on a farm or as a craftsman's apprentice in return for passage to America and room and board. When the first Africans arrived in the then-British colonies during the 17th century, some colonists thought that they should be treated as indentured servants, too. Eventually, the question of whether the Africans should be considered indentured, like the Englishmen, or slaves who could be owned for life, was considered in a Maryland court. The court's calamitous decree held that blacks were slaves bound to lifelong servitude, and so were their children. America went through a time of moral examination and civil war pitting brother against brother before it finally freed African slaves, as well as their descendants. The principle that all men are created equal had faced its greatest challenge and survived.

The court ruling that set blacks apart from other races fanned flames of discrimination that lasted long after slavery was abolished. The concept of racism had existed for centuries in countries throughout the world. When the Manchus conquered China in the 17th century, they decreed that Chinese and Manchus could not intermarry. To impress their superiority on the conquered Chinese, the Manchus ordered all Chinese men to wear their hair in a long braid called a queue.

By the 19th century, some intellectuals took up the banner of racism, citing Charles Darwin's work on the evolution of animals as proof of their position. Darwin's studies theorized that highly evolved animals were dominant over other animals. Some advocates of this theory applied it to humans, asserting that certain races were more highly evolved than others and thus were superior.

This philosophy served as the basis for a new discrimination, not only against certain races, but also against various ethnic groups. These ugly ideas were directed at black people and other victims as well. Asians faced harsh discrimination and were depicted by 19th-century newspaper cartoonists who chronicled public opinion as depraved, degenerate people, deficient in intelligence. When the Irish flooded American cities to escape the famine in Ireland, the cartoonists caricatured the typical "Paddy" (a popular term for Irish immigrants) as an apelike creature with jutting jaw and sloping forehead.

By the 20th century, these concepts of racism and ethnic prejudice had developed into virulent theories of a Northern European master race. When Adolf Hitler came to power in Germany in 1933, he popularized the notion of Aryan supremacy. "Aryan," a term referring to the Indo-European races, was applied to so-called superior physical characteristics such as blond hair, blue eyes, and delicate facial features. Anyone with darker and heavier features was considered inferior. Buttressed by these theories, the German Nazi state from 1933 to 1945 set out to destroy European Jews, along with Gypsies and other groups considered inferior. It nearly succeeded. Millions of these people were killed.

How supremely important it is, then, that we have learned to live with one another, respecting differences while treasuring the things we share.

A relatively recent example of this nonviolent way of resolving differences is the solution the Canadians found to a conflict between two ethnic groups. The conflict arose in the mid-1960s between the peoples of French-speaking Quebec Province and those of the English-speaking provinces. Relations grew tense, then bitter, then violent. The Royal Commission on Bilingualism and Biculturalism was established to study the growing crisis and to propose measures to ease the tensions. As a result of the commission's recommendations, all official documents and statements from the national government's capital at Ottawa are now issued in both French and English, and bilingual education is encouraged.

The year 1980 marked a coming of age for the United States' ethnic heritage. For the first time, the U.S. Census asked people about their ethnic background. Americans chose from more than 100 groups, including French, Basque, Spanish Basque,

French Canadian, Afro-American, Peruvian, Armenian, Chinese, and Japanese, among others. The ethnic group with the largest response was English (49.6 million). More than 100 million Americans claimed ancestors from the British Isles, which includes Ireland, Wales, and Scotland. There were almost as many Germans (49.2 million) as English. The Irish-American population (40.2 million) was third, but the next largest ethnic group, the Afro-Americans, was a distant fourth (21 million). There was a sizable group of French ancestry (13 million), as well as of Italian (12 million). Poles, Dutch, Swedes, Norwegians, and Russians followed. These groups, and other smaller ones, represent the wondrous profusion of ethnic influences in North America.

Canada, too, has discovered the diversity of its population. Studies conducted during the French/English conflict determined that Canadians were descended from Ukrainians, Germans, Italians, Chinese, Japanese, native Indians, and Eskimos. Canada found it had no ethnic majority, although nearly half of its immigrant population came from the British Isles. Canada, like the United States, is a land of immigrants for whom mutual tolerance is a matter of reason as well as principle. Tolerance is a virtue that has brought North America peace.

The people of North America are the descendants of one of the greatest migrations in history. That migration is not over. Koreans, Vietnamese, Nicaraguans, and Cubans are heading for the shores of North America in large numbers. This mix of cultures shapes every aspect of our lives. To understand ourselves, we must know something about our ethnic ancestry, as well as about the ancestry of others, because in a sense, they are part of our history, too. Nothing so defines the North American nations as the motto on the Great Seal of the United States: *E Pluribus Unum*—Out of Many, One.

Acknowledgments *(continued from p. ii)*

Merlyn's Pen, Inc.

"i am kwakkoli" by Bisco Hill, from *Merlyn's Pen: Fiction, Essays, and Poems by America's Teens*. Copyright by Merlyn's Pen, Inc. All Rights Reserved. Reprinted by permission of Merlyn's Pen, Inc.

Nellie Wong

"Where Is My Country?" by Nellie Wong, published in *Chinese American Poetry: An Anthology*, edited by L. Ling-Chi Wang and Henry Yiheng Zhao, University of Washington Press, © 1987 by Nellie Wong. Reprinted by permission of the author.

Note: Every effort has been made to locate the copyright owner of material reprinted in this book. Omissions brought to our attention will be corrected in subsequent editions.